Also by Sarah A. Chrisman:

Historical Fiction:
First Wheel in Town
Love Will Find A Wheel
A Rapping at the Door
Delivery Delayed

Non-fiction:
Victorian Secrets
This Victorian Life

Anthologies:
Love's Messenger
Words for Parting
A Christmas Wish
The Wheelman's Joy
True Ladies and Proper Gentlemen

Quotations of Quality

A Commonplace Book of Victorian Advice, Wit, and Observations on Life

Compiled and edited by
Sarah A. Chrisman

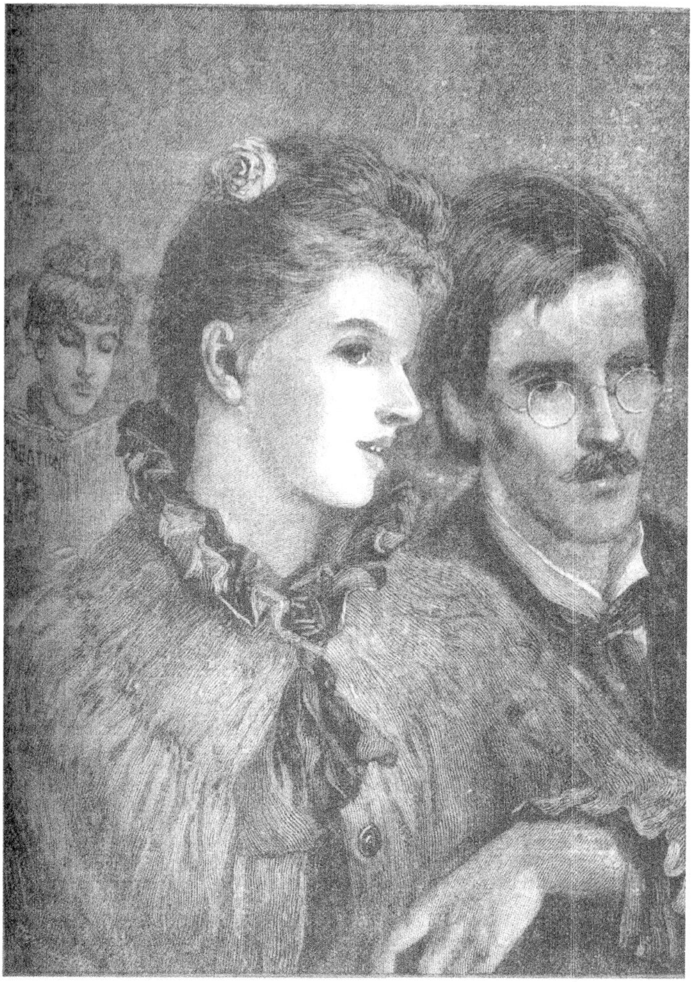

Contents

Introduction…p. 8

Commonplace Books…p. 10

Books…p. 12

Writing…p. 31

Language…p. 43

Publishers… p. 48

Encouragement and Perseverance…p. 52

Optimism…p. 58

Happiness…p. 61

Women…p. 63

Men…p. 71

The Sexes…p. 75

Love…p. 83

Home…p. 86

Time…p. 92

History…p. 97

Memory…p. 101

Education…p. 103

Health…p. 109

Imagination…p. 113

Art…p. 117

Fashion…p. 120

Food…p. 126

Work…p. 129

Money…p. 138

Technology…p. 140

Politics…p. 142

The Company We Keep…p. 145

Minding your own business…p. 153

Miscellaneous…p. 155

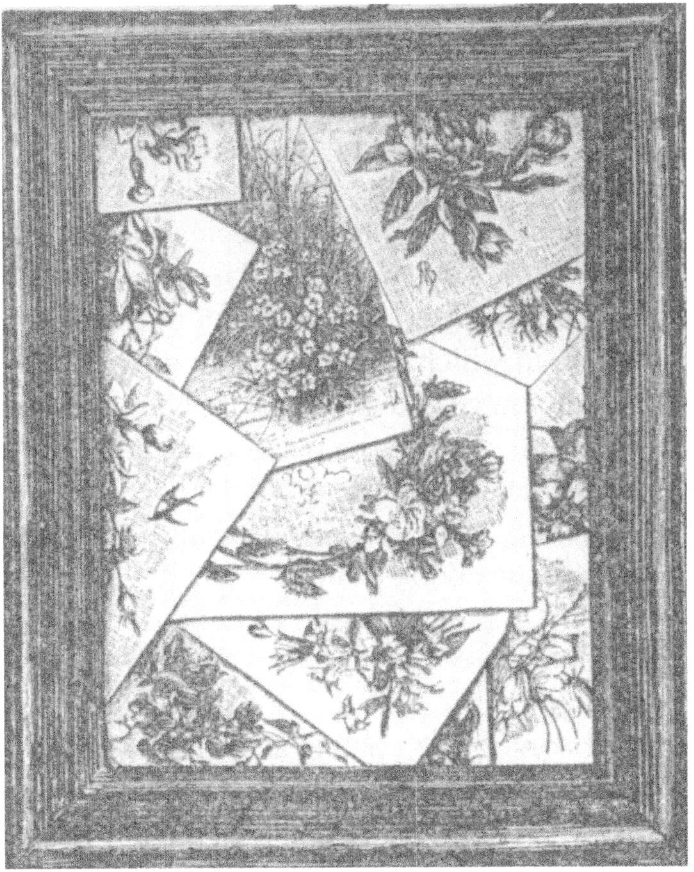

Introduction

Commonplace books —volumes holding many quotes from a number of different sources— have an ancient history, predating the Common Era. They are essentially the literary equivalent of a floral bouquet, in which blossoms from many different sources are brought together to be appreciated in a single location common to all of them —i.e., a common place.

The Victorians were especially fond of commonplace books, and this particular compilation is a collection of quotations from Victorian sources. By representing sentiments expressed during that time on a number of topics, it paints an impressionist portrait of the era in the eloquent words of those who lived through it.

If this particular collection of quotes seems a bit heavy on books and writing it is for a very simple reason: it was compiled by a writer. It is only natural that a bouquet's fragrance should be influenced by tastes of the lady who picked and assembled the blossoms. The statements herein go beyond mere wordcraft, however. There is something both universal and timeless about the ideas in

this volume. May they bring you as much inspiration and provoke as many rewarding discussions with your friends for you as they have done for me.
 —*S.C.*

Commonplace Books

"I would also commend the practice of copying into a blank book, such passages from your reading as forcibly strike your mind, or as you think may prove especially serviceable to dwell upon, or to use at some future time."
—W.H. Venable, 1872.
The National Teacher, October, 1872. p. 382.

***

"A commonplace book 'may, like conversation with a friend, open up sources of sympathy and reflection; excite to argument, agreement, or disagreement; and, like every spontaneous utterance of thought out of an earnest mind, suggest far higher and better thoughts than any to be found here to higher and more productive minds.'"
—Mrs. Jameson, 1877.
A Common-Place Book of Thoughts, Memories, and Fancies. London: Virtue and Company, 1877. p. vi.

***

"When we hear of an 'anthology' we always think of a collection of poems, but of course the thought is not inevitable; it is only the result of constant association, for there are

beautiful and precious things of verse. More than once it has occurred to me what a charming volume might be made by some leisured reader of good fiction, who would go through the volumes of some of our best writers and collect from them the isolated utterances of noble sentiment or profound reflection, which…have really an independent life and value. The mere novel-devourer, eager for 'the story,' misses them altogether; the more careful reader notes and enjoys them, but unless he is young enough or old-fashioned enough to keep a commonplace book, they soon slip into the limbo of things forgotten; whereas, could they find a permanent separateness on the printed page of an anthology, they could be returned to again and again."
—Anonymous, 1894.
The Leisure Hour, 1894, p. 323.
***

"Bees and birds that are not poets go the round of the world's gardens, stealing from flowers and fruits to make their honey and song, and never a creature says 'Stop thief!'"
—Anonymous, 1894.
The Leisure Hour, 1894. p. 46.
***

Books

"Judicious, well directed reading, which is study, teaches what life is, what the world is, and better fits a man for every duty and occupation he enters in, it broadens his views and makes him more competent."
—Warner, Charles Dudley, 1896.
"Literature in the Home." *Good Housekeeping*, January, 1896, p. 10.
***

"The taste for reading and the habit of reading must always be developed from within; they can never be added from without."
—Charles F. Richardson, 1881.
The Choice of Books, 1881, p. 5.
***

"Books are as much a part of a home as pictures or furniture or carpets."
—Walter R. Houghton, 1889.
American Etiquette and Rules of Politeness. 1889, p. 50.
***

"What a *facination* there is in really good reading! What a *power* it gives one!"
—John S. Hart, 1885.

Bancroft's Fifth Reader, 1885, p. 192.
***

"To be able to judge what is good reading, requires one to be a good reader."
—Annie Randall White, 1891.
Polite Society at Home and Abroad, 1891. p. 430.
***

"It is an excellent thing for every young person of literary inclination to begin early the collection of a private library. I do not see why women should not make this an object in life."
—W.H. Venable, 1872.
"Something About Libraries, Books, and Reading."
The National Teacher. October, 1872, p. 379.
***

"My dearest comrade, my chosen friend is the girl who loves to read. I am thankful that there are so many of her."
—Ruth Ashmore, 1893.
The Ladies' Home Journal, December, 1893, p. 20.
***

"Many homes are conspicuous by the absence of books. A few fancifully-bound volumes may be found, a daily paper, and now and

then a magazine. In these homes young minds are starved."
—Annie Randall White, 1891.
Polite Society at Home and Abroad, 1891. p. 431.
***

"[T]he healthy and hungry mind will, by a wonderful instinct and adaptation to nature, commonly select for its own good and pleasure that reading which, by the verdict of the world's experience, is permanently valuable."
—W.H. Venable, 1872.
"Something About Libraries, Books, and Reading."
The National Teacher. October, 1872, p. 380.
***

"Every home should start a small library, to which additions can be made continually."
—Annie Randall White, 1891.
Polite Society at Home and Abroad, 1891. p. 431.
***

"Sometimes we do not fully realize the profit from a book until long after we have finished the reading of it."
—W.H. Venable, 1872.
"Something About Libraries, Books, and Reading."
The National Teacher. October, 1872, p. 382.
***

"The boy who loves books and cons the pages of good ones faithfully, drawing in lessons of truth and experience to serve as guides, is better prepared for the contact with the hard places of life, than the boy who cares nothing for them, and who has gathered no instruction from their silent teachings. A reading people is always a thinking people."
—Annie Randall White, 1891.
Polite Society at Home and Abroad, 1891. p. 438.
***

"If a person has not much desire for reading, the little taste they have can be cultivated, and intellectual improvement will come easily. The mind that never receives a new idea becomes stunted and dwarfed."
—Annie Randall White, 1891.
Polite Society at Home and Abroad, 1891. p. 431.
***

"There is a pretty large number of books, chiefly belletristic, that every person who claims a place in cultivated society, is presumed by his associates to have read."
—W.H. Venable, 1872.
"Something About Libraries, Books, and Reading."
The National Teacher. October, 1872, p. 381.
***

"The habit of reading and comparing a knowledge of what has been done and said before, of the experiments that have been tried in the past, make a man a better observer and judge of what is going on about him. By this knowledge he is better fitted to perform his duties as a citizen."
—Charles Dudley Warner, 1896.
"Literature in the Home." *Good Housekeeping*, January, 1896, p. 10.
***

"Where the reading ends the thinking should begin with renewed intensity."
—W.H. Venable, 1872.
"Something About Libraries, Books, and Reading." *The National Teacher.* October, 1872, p. 382.
***

"All that mankind has done, thought, gained, or been; it is lying as in magic preservation in the pages of books."
—Thomas Carlyle, 1846.
On Heroes, Hero-Worship and the Heroic in History. New York: Wiley and Putnam, 1846. p. 143.
***

"A minute's reading often provokes a day's thinking."

—W.H. Venable, 1872.
"Something About Libraries, Books, and Reading."
The National Teacher. October, 1872, p. 382.
***

"In his love for knowledge and familiarity with books a man may find his happiness and usefulness increased a hundred fold."
—Walter R. Houghton, 1889.
American Etiquette and Rules of Politeness. 1889, p. 33-34.
***

"One *may* understand and not read well; no one can read well and not understand."
—W.H. Venable, 1872.
"Something About Libraries, Books, and Reading."
The National Teacher. October, 1872, p. 382.
***

"Books are the windows through which the mind looks out."
—Anonymous, 1889.
Zion's Home Monthly, January 15, 1889. p. 197.
***

"A house without books is like a room without windows."
—Henry Ward Beecher, 1862.
Eyes and Ears, 1862, p. 146.

***

"A home without books is desolate indeed."
—Walter R. Houghton, 1889.
American Etiquette and Rules of Politeness. 1889, p. 50.
***

"Life being short, and the quiet hours of it few, we ought to waste none of them in reading valueless books; and valuable books should, in a civilized country, be within reach of everyone, printed in excellent form, for a just price."
—John Ruskin, 1878.
Pearls for Young Ladies, 1878, p. 18.
***

"With the boundless facilities for reading the best and worst literature, with the vast strides that the "art preservative" has made in furnishing the homes and libraries with books from the "unabridged" down to a child's primer, it seems an easy task to decide what shall be read. And yet to sift out the worthless, from among this mass, leaving the valuable for perusal, is no light undertaking, and one whose importance is vast."
—Annie Randall White, 1891.

Polite Society at Home and Abroad, 1891. p. 430.
***

"The books we read should be chosen with great care, that they may be, as an Egyptian king wrote over his library, "The medicines of the soul."
—Paxton Hood, 19th-century.
A Dictionary of Thoughts., 1891. p. 48.
***

"Books are the metempsychosis; the symbol and presage of immortality. —The dead are scattered, and none shall find them; but behold they are here. They do but sleep. At your summons every one shall speak and instruct you in the best experiences of his life!"
—Henry Ward Beecher, 1868.
Norwood: Or, Village Life in New England, 1868, p. 71.
***

"A good book is the purest essence of a human soul."
— Thomas Carlyle, 1840.
"Speech At Freemason's Tavern, June 24, 1840." *Life of Thomas Carlyle*, London: W.H. Allen & Co., 1881. p. 218.
***

"To *know* one good book well, is better than to know something *about* a hundred good books, at second hand."
—Charles F. Richardson, 1881.
The Choice of Books, 1881, p. 5.
***

"All books have an atmosphere of their own. They suggest much more than they contain."
—Hester M. Poole, 1889.
"Books: Selection, Arrangement and Use of Them."
Good Housekeeping. October 12, 1889. p. 272.
***

"Read I must, or I shall starve."
"What nonsense you are talking, Marcia!" good Mrs. Austin had answered, severely. "It's real sinful to talk in that way, about starving for want of books, when you have plenty of good victuals to eat."
Marcia had answered, quietly, "There are different kinds of starvation"".
—Maggie T. Sutherland, 1877.
"The Day of the Picnic." *Petersen's Magazine,* June, 1877, p. 437.
***

"Books and desk are essentials, "meat and drink," and wherever most convenient for use, would be best."
—Anonymous, 1883.
"Queries," *Table Talk*, November, 1883, p. 390.
***

"No book worth reading ever fails to be steeped with the spirit of the person who wrote it."
—P.L. Ford, 1897.
The Story of An Untold Love, 1897, pp. 262—263.
***

"You see they've every one [of these written texts] got something to say to us. Every one's going to talk and be like a living thing these long nights and days when there's no one else to make a sound."
—Mrs. I.T. Hopkins, 1887.
Arrow Head Light, 1887, p. 59.
***

"Books are standing counselors and preachers, always at hand, and always disinterested; having this advantage over oral instructors, that they are ready to repeat their lesson as often as we please."
—Chambers, 1858.

Young Men's Magazine, January, 1858, p. 416.
***

"Be as careful of the books you read, as the company you keep, for your habits and character will be as much influenced by the former as the latter."
—Paxton Hood, 19th-century
Polite Society at Home and Abroad, 1891. p. 438.
***

"It is chiefly through books that we enjoy intercourse with superior minds, and these invaluable means of communication are within the reach of all. In the best books great men talk to us, give us their most precious thoughts, and pour their souls into ours. God be thanked for books. They are the voices of the distant and the dead, and make us heirs of the spiritual life of past ages. Books are the true levelers. They give to all, who will faithfully use them, the society, the spiritual presence of the best and greatest of our race. No matter how poor I am,—no matter though the prosperous of my own time will not enter my obscure dwelling,—if sacred writers will enter and take up their abode under my roof,—if Milton will cross my threshold and sing to me of Paradise, and Shakespeare to

open to me the worlds of imagination and the workings of the human heart, and Franklin to enrich me with his practical wisdom, I shall not pine for want of intellectual companionship, and I may become a cultivated man, though excluded from what is called the best society in the place where I live."
—Channing, 1883.
"Books." *Bancroft's Fifth Reader,* 1883. p. 300.
***

"Except a living man there is nothing more wonderful than a book! A message to us from the dead —from human souls we never saw, who lived, perhaps, thousands of miles away. And yet these, in those little sheets of paper, speak to us, arouse us, terrify us, teach us, comfort us, open their hearts to us as brothers."
—Charles Kingsley, 19th-century.
A Dictionary of Thoughts., 1891. p. 47.
***

"What is a book? A book is brains boiled down, distilled and mixed with printer's ink. A book means civilization. It means language fixed and frozen, carved into immortal beauty… A book is a garden; an orchard, a

storehouse; it is company by the way; it is a counselor. Books are those faithful mirrors that reflect to our minds the minds of sages and heroes. A good book is the precious life-blood of a master spirit treasured up on a purpose for a life beyond."
—J.F. Spaunhurst, 1896.
Missouri School Journal, March, 1896, p. 133.
***

"Books are among the best friends that it is possible for any man to have. They will be silent when he does not wish to converse, they will speak to him when he desires to be spoken to; they will take no offence at his silence, neither will they take any offence at all at his comments. They include the most illustrious of the living and the most illustrious of the dead. Having books, a man can number among his friends those who have distinguished themselves in civil life and in military life; he can have friends from the state, he can have friends from the church. He can entertain them all his life at the least possible expense, because they ask no more at his hands than the tenderest accomodations and the quietest place in his dwelling."
—Rev. John Hall, D.D. 1885.
The Book of Best Things. 1885, pp. 18—19.

***

"To use books rightly, is to go to them for help; to appeal to them when our own knowledge and power fail; to be led by them into wider sight and purer conception than our own, and to receive from them the united sentence of the judges and councils of all time, against our solitary and unstable opinions."
—John Ruskin, 1883.
Sesame and Lilies, 1883, p. 59.
***

"A little library, growing every year, is an honorable part of a young man's history. It is a man's duty to have books. A library is not a luxury, but one of the necessaries of life."
—Anonymous, 1889.
Zion's Home Monthly, January 15, 1889. p. 198.
***

"No man has a right to bring up his children without surrounding them with books, if he has the means to buy them. It is a wrong to his family. He cheats them!"
—Anonymous, 1889.
Zion's Home Monthly, January 15, 1889. p. 197.
***

"Among the earliest ambitions to be excited in clerks, workmen, journeymen, and indeed, among all that are struggling up in life from nothing to something, is that of owning, and constantly adding to, a library of good books."
—Anonymous, 1889.
Zion's Home Monthly, January 15, 1889. p. 198.
***

"We hear a great deal said in these days about 'books that have helped me,' books that have come to us and spoken to us as a brother would do, books that have revealed to us powers and possibilities in our own souls that we had never dreamed of. These are not always the books that our literature critics judge to be the greatest, but they are books that our hearts pronounce good. We love them, we read them again and again; and they help us."
—Rev. A.B. Curtis, 1890.
"Thoughts That Have Helped Me", *The Unitarian*, February, 1890, p. 57.
***

"The books that help you most, are those which make you think the most, —The hardest way of learning is that of easy

reading; but a great book that comes from a great thinker is a ship of thought, deep freighted with truth and beauty."
—Theodore Parker, 1891.
A Dictionary of Thoughts, 1891. p. 49.
***

"The library at Windygates was the largest and the handsomest room in the house. The two grand divisions under which Literature is usually arranged in these days occupied the customary places in it. On the shelves which ran round the walls were the books which humanity in general respects —and does not read. On the tables distributed over the floor were the books which humanity which humanity in general reads —and does not respect."
—Wilkie Collins, 1870.
Man and Wife. 1870, p. 258.
***

"A book is not bad because it fails to please 'all and some.' If it pleases some who are worthy of being detached from the all, it is good. A case in physics may help to illustrate this fact. A body is not unmagnetic because it fails to attract all things; it is magnetic if it attact iron."

—Anonymous, 1894.
"Second Thoughts on Books." *Leisure Hour*, 1894, p. 46.
***

"The best books for a man are not always those which the wise recommend, but often those which meet the peculiar wants, the natural thirst of his mind, and therefore awaken and rivet thought."
—Dr. Channing, 1872.
"On Self Culture." *Barnard's American Journal of Education*, 1872, p. 207.
***

"The first step is to establish a regulated economy of your time, so that without interference with a due attention to business and to health, you may get two clear hours every day for reading of the best kind. It is not much, some men would tell you that it is not enough, but I purposely fix the expenditure of time at a low figure because I want it to be practicable consistently with all the duties and necessary pleasures of your life."
—Philip Gilbert Hamerton, 1885.
The Intellectual Life, 1885, p. 204.
***

"To give an account of one's reading is in some sort to give an account of one's life."
—William Dean Howells, 1893.
"My Literary Passions." *The Ladies' Home Journal*, December 1893, p. 10.
***

"The very first thing to be remembered by him who would study the art of reading is that nothing can take the place of personal enthusiasm and personal work."
—Charles F. Richardson, 1881.
The Choice of Books, 1881, p. 5.
***

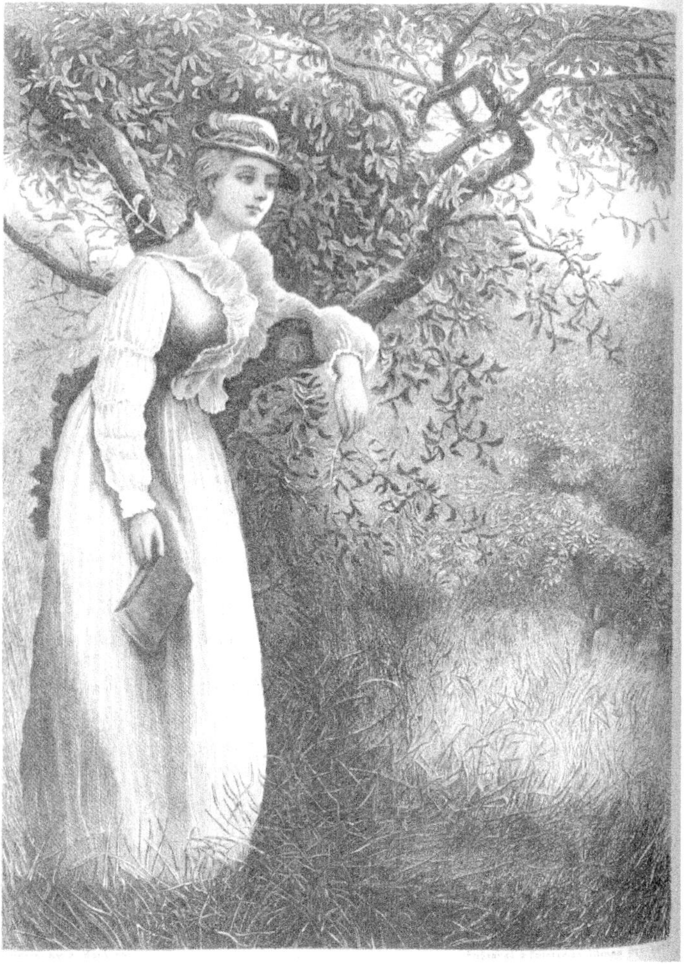

Writing

"The author himself must live through what he describes."
—Wolstan Dixey, 1889.
The Trade of Authorship, 1889. p. 111.
***

"Every new book must have, in the consciousness of its author, a private history that, like the mysteries of romance, would if unfolded have an interest for the reader, and by unveiling the inner life of the volume show its character and tendencies."
—Sarah Josepha Hale, 1866.
Manners, 1866, p. 3.
***

"The author is, as we must ever remember, of peculiar organisation. He is a being born with a predisposition which with him is irresistible, the bent of which he cannot in any way avoid, whether it directs him to the abstruse researches of erudition or induces him to mount into the fervid and turbulent atmosphere of imagination."
—Benjamin Disraeli, 1868.

"Speech at Royal Literary Fund Dinner, May 6, 1868." *Wit and Wisdom of Benjamin Disraeli*, 1880, p. 16.
***

"An author is a solitary being, who, for the same reason he pleases one, must consequently displease another."
—Isaac Disraeli, 1859.
Literary Character of Men of Genius. 1859, p. 301.
***

"The pen is the tongue of the hand: a silent utterer of words for the eye."
—Henry Ward Beecher, 1862.
Eyes and Ears, 1862, p. 245.
***

"If a book come from the heart it will contrive to reach other hearts.—All art and authorcraft are of small account to that."
—Thomas Carlyle, 19th-century.
A Dictionary of Thoughts, 1891. p. 47.
***

"What won me a little, too, was the fact that the scene she was reciting…was secretly my favorite among all the sketches from my pen… I never said so, but it was; and I had

always felt a wondering annoyance that the…public, while kindly praising beyond their worth other attempts of mine, had never noticed the higher purpose of this little shaft, aimed not at the balconies and lighted windows of society, but straight up towards the distant stars."
—Constance Fenimore Woolson, 1880.
"Miss Grief." *Lippincott's Monthly Magazine*, May, 1880, p. 576.
***

"Now I will be anything else if you please except dull. You may say I have been dull already? As I am an honest woman, I don't agree with you. There are some people who bring dull minds to their reading, and then blame the writer for it. I say no more."
—Wilkie Collins, 1872.
Poor Miss Finch. 1872, p. 501.
***

"A misprint kills a sensitive author. An intentional change of his text murders him. No wonder so many poets die young!"
—Oliver Wendell Holmes, 1887.
The Autocrat of the Breakfast Table, 1887, p. 31.
***

"If a woman is born with a talent to write she will write —there is no possible doubt about that."
—Rayne, 1883.
What Can A Woman Do? 1883, p. 47.
***

"A book stands very much in the same relation to a writer that a baby does to its mother."
—P.L. Ford, 1899.
The Story of An Untold Love, Boston: Houghton, Mifflin & Company, 1899, p. 262.
***

"To think clearly is the first requisite [to writing]; the next, to clear expression to the thought. A good ear, a sound judgement, and a thorough knowledge of English grammar, —all contribute."
—John Tyndall, 1893.
Journal of Education, August 17, 1893. p. 114.
***

"Young authors should cultivate their minds, and let their style take care of itself."
—Jean Ingelow, 1893.
Journal of Education, August 17, 1893. p. 114.
***

"When one has something to say, — something he must express, —he will say it in his natural and special way; and his way forms his style, and the style is thus the man."
—E.C. Stedman, 1893.
Journal of Education, August 17, 1893. p. 114.
***

"My own style is the result of down-right hard work. This, and the experience of life, have been my chief teachers."
—Elizabeth Stuart Phelps, 1893.
Journal of Education, August 17, 1893. p. 114.
***

"Don't undertake too large a field. Better tell everything about something than something about everything."
—Wolstan Dixey, 1888.
The Trade of Authorship, 1888, p. 81.
***

"It is a great advance in civilization to be able to describe the common facts of life, and perhaps, if we were to examine it, we should find that it was at least an equal advance to wish to describe them."
—Walter Bagehot, 1872.

Physics and Politics. 1872, p. 212.
***

"It is a capital plan to carry a tablet with you and, when you find yourself felicitous, take notes of your own conversation."
—Oliver Wendell Holmes, 1875.
The Autocrat of the Breakfast Table, 1875, p. vi.
***

"Eloquence delights in long sentences, wit in short."
—Anonymous, 1850.
Harper's New Monthly Magazine, July, 1850, p. 148.
***

"A single fact is worth a folio of argument."
—Freeman Hunt, 1856.
Worth and Wealth, 1856, p. 217.
***

"Billings give four rules —which may well be known as Golden— for the preparation of an article for a journal:
1. Have something to say.
2. Say it.
3. Stop as soon as you have said it.
4. Give the paper a proper title.
—Anonymous, 1881.

The Ohio Medical Journal, October, 1881, p. 192.
***

"The eloquent descriptions and the striking reflections are just the parts of a story-book that people never read. Whatever we do, let us not, if we can possibly help it, write so much as a single sentence that can be conveniently skipped."
—Wilkie Collins, Collins,
After Dark, 1856, p. 28.
***

"In the work of great painters and writers you have probably observed that sometimes they create "impressions" without giving all the details. Young writers are prone to think it is a sign of genius to neglect details and jump immediately at broad generalizations and sweeping effects. Beginners want to be "impressionists" at the start. Very good if they *could* be; it is high art, but they must come up to it step by step. Only the artist that has carefully and minutely studied the leaf and the twig can make that broad stroke with his thumb, which, viewed across the room, passes successfully for a tree. Only one who has observed life closely in its details knows how to select those telling features that so

graphically suggest all the rest. Only those who have *seen everything* —and could put everything in if they chose— know just what they may safely leave out… You must *realize* before you can idealize; you must know the facts and know them intimately before you can gather them together to paint a moral or adorn a tale."
———Wolstan Dixey, 1888.
The Trade of Authorship, 1888, p. 86.
***

"We are now in the very midst of a well-dressed and well mannered set of women who work at their pen as Penelope at her web."
—Rayne, 1883.
What Can A Woman Do? 1883, p. 414.
***

"A great writer does not reveal himself here and there, but everywhere."
—James Russell Lowell, 1871.
My Study Windows, 1871, p. 261.
***

"Let me here correct an impression that seems to prevail extensively as to the rewards of literary life. It certainly has its rewards, and of the most delightful kind… But so far as

literature pays cash down it is not to be compared to —shoemaking, for instance."
—Gail Hamilton, 1870.
A Battle of the Books, 1870, pp. 267—268.
***

"What a wonderful, what an almost magical boon, a writer of great genius confers upon us, when we read him intelligently. As he proceeds from point to point in his argument or narrative, we seem to be taken up by him, and carried from hill-top to hill-top, where, through an atmosphere of light, we survey a glorious region of thought, looking freely, far and wide, above and below, and gazing in admiration upon all the beauty and grandeur of the scene."
—Horace Mann, 19th-century.
Life and Works of Horace Mann, 1891, p. 305.
***

"I never saw an author in my life… that did not purr as audibly as a full-grown domestic cat on having his fur smoothed the right way by a skilful hand."
—Oliver Wendell Holmes, 1887.
The Autocrat of the Breakfast Table, 1887, p. 31.
***

"Two sorts of writers possess genius: those who think, and those who cause others to think."
—Joseph Roux, 1886.
Meditations of a Parish Priest, 1886, p. 12.
***

"It is action that discovers the rules for action; only through experience with *things* and *facts* are principles acquired."
—Wolstan Dixey, 1888.
The Trade of Authorship, 1888, p. 81.
***

"Facts, facts, facts; there *is* nothing but facts. The writer's first busines is to get at these facts exactly —get the meat out of them— and then, *by the most direct method*, to transmit them to his readers. That is the whole substructure of literature; the groundwork —the anatomy."
—Wolstan Dixey.
The Trade of Authorship, 1888, p. 83.
***

"Learn to *see* well and *hear* well. Have all your senses sharpened so that you may perceive thing *as they are*, not as other people tell you they are… Then these *perceptions*

will give you *ideas* (that is if you are capable of ideas). Then come *words;* but the words must never come first. Words are only paper currency: every one must bear the stamp of an idea, else it is counterfeit; and must have a golden fact behind it, ready to redeem it, else it is worthless."
——Wolstan Dixey, 1888.
The Trade of Authorship, 1888, p. 83.
***

"She advanced to writing notes; and from writing notes to keeping a journal —this last at the suggestion of her aunt, who had lived in the days before penny postage, when people kept journals and wrote long letters; in short, when people had time to think of themselves, and, more wonderful still, to write about it, too."
—Wilkie Collins, 1872.
Poor Miss Finch, 1872, p. 501.
***

"In introducing a new idea to your reader remember that the human mind proceeds from the known to the unknown. The imagination *remembers half* and multiplies it by two, or four, or ten, or whatever it may be. The imagination can easily multiply when it

knows a fraction of an idea, but *it can never guess at half.*"
—Wolstan Dixey, 1888.
The Trade of Authorship, 1888, p. 80.
***

Language

"To me, words are a mystery and a marvel…
There is no point where art so nearly touches
nature as when it appears in the form of
words."
—J.G. Holland, 1884.
Plain Talks on Familiar Subjects. 1884, p. 287.
***

"Words are freeborn, and not the vassals of
the gruff tyrants of prose to do their bidding
only. They have the same right to dance and
sing as the dewdrops have to sparkle and the
stars to shine."
—Abraham Coles, 1882.
The Evangel, 1882. p. xvii.
***

"Thoughts come maimed and plucked of
plumage from the lips, which, from the pen,
in the silence of your own leisure and study,
would be born with far more beauty."
—Lady Blessington, 19th-century.
A Dictionary of Thoughts, 1891. p. 639.
***

"Words are a delight to me, as colors are to a painter."
—Louise Chandler Moulton, 1893.
Journal of Education, August 17, 1893. p. 114.
***

"In the *first* place, we obtain from the forms and scenes and processes of nature no small part of all our language. The word spirit, which now signifies the very opposite of matter, meant originally breath or wind, this being the natural symbol of an unseen force. Words now expressing states of the soul, like sincerity (from *sine cera*, without wax, concealing cracks or flaws in Roman pottery, or without wax in honey —in one case a sincere vase and in the other sincere honey), had their origin in material forms or processes. Take again, the word conspiracy, a breathing together of persons engaged in secret whispered consultation. In order, therefore, to understand language properly, it is necessary to know those prior meanings of words which refer to objects and movements that pertain to the outward and material realm of being."
—Prof. E.B. Andrews, 1872.
"Nature the Teacher of Childhood." *The National Teacher.* June, 1872, pp. 188—189.

***

"The [Ancient] Greeks said that barbarians did not speak, they twittered."
—Charles DeKay, 1898.
Bird Gods, 1898. p. 49.
***

"If your every-day language is not fit for a letter or for print, it is not fit for talk."
—Edward Everett Hale, 1885.
Bancroft's Fifth Reader, 1885, p, 85.
***

"I am going to get up a Society for Prevention of Cruelty to Prepositions. Animals have certain natural means of defence. They can bite, and prepositions cannot."
—Russell Lowell, 1894.
The Leisure Hour, 1894, p. 524.
***

"Wearing diamonds does not exempt one from being careful about their verbs."
—K.H.T., 1893.
Good Housekeeping, February, 1893, p. 101.
***

"To talk well and wisely is a great power, and many people greatly influence society by their power of expression."
—Rev. A.D. Mayo, 1872.
"The Spirit of School Discipline." *The National Teacher*, February, 1872, p. 45.

***

"Vivid conceptions are the life and inspiration of the orator, and the power of being vivid, the power of giving such projection or outwardness to a scene or picture illustrating and enforcing some great truth or principle, and without which no orator can sway his audience, is derived only from those habits of observing outward nature formed in very early years."
—Prof. E.B. Andrews, 1872.
"Nature the Teacher of Childhood." *The National Teacher.* June, 1872, p. 192.

***

"Every occupation gives origin to peculiar similies. A farmer speaking of his neighbor's embarrassed circumstances and inability to extricate himself from surrounding difficulties compared him to *a toad under a harrow.*"
—Anonymous, 1872.
The National Teacher, February, 1872, p. 59.

***

"Observe carefully; persist in selecting the word that describes exactly what you want to describe; not something pretty near to it. Every time you use a word which is almost what you want but not quite, the outline of the picture at that point becomes blurred and indistinct."
—Wolstan Dixey, 1888.
The Trade of Authorship, 1888, p. 84.
***

Publishers

"It seems to me, also, that there is no business in which so few checks exist as that of publishing. An author...has literally nothing but the publisher's word by which to know how many copies are sold... Of course a false return of sales would be fraud, and somewhat complicated fraud; but human ingenuity combined with human depravity has been known to surmount obstacles to crime as formidable as these, and the danger of detection is infinitessimally small... If a publisher may for years safely disregard, not to say violate, the condition of a contract which an author has before his eyes in black and white, how long before another publisher falsifies accounts?"
—Gail Hamilton, 1870.
A Battle of the Books, 1870, pp. 254—255.
***

"I believe there is some solid foundation for the complaint of authors against publishers taking the lion's share of the profits; and that the time is right upon us when the majority of authors will take matters into their own hands with a little business shrewdness, and

balancing the profits with the losses will come out ahead as the publishers now do… If you want the lion's share, be the lion."
—Wolstan Dixey, 1888.
The Trade of Authorship, 1888, pp. 53, 57.
***

"It does seem that there ought to be some way, with all the books that are read—good, bad, and indifferent—for the authors of them to get some sort of proportionate cash payment…when people…want to read and pay for it, it seems that the larger proportion of the cash should go into the pocket of the author, and I do believe that if the majority of authors who are now making fortunes for publishers would only have a little business common sense and courage, they would get pay more nearly commensurate with their share of the work."
—Wolstan Dixey, 1888.
The Trade of Authorship, New York: Wolstan Dixey. 1888, p. 52.
***

"I do not see why the publisher's profits need be considered as the ultima Thule of an author's. Is it the phantom of a distorted imagination that the author has a far larger

property in the book than the publisher? Does it not cost him infinitely more than it costs the publisher? And even leaving the infinite, and coming down to finite matters, are not the fields which the publisher reaps so much broader than the author's one little close, that a far smaller share in the gleanings would give a publisher a far more heaping granary. An author, we will say, publishes one book in a year. His profits are a thousand dollars. But the publisher publishes twenty books a year, on which, in the same ratio, he gets twenty thousand dollars."
—Gail Hamilton, 1870.
The Battle of the Books, 1870, pp. 120—127.
***

"[B]etween an author, who has spent years on a book, and the average critic, who is at best superficial in his knowledge of a subject, the former is the more often right of the two."
—Ford, P.L.
The Story of An Untold Love, 1897, p. 198.
***

"In controversies with publishers, the author is at a signal disadvantage by reason of the connection of publishers with the press. Publishers have the entrée of the newspapers

by their advertising, and all in the way of business, it is the easiest thing in the world to give public opinion a tilt in the desired direction without the least suspicion on the part of the reader."
—Gail Hamilton, 1870.
A Battle of the Books, 1870, p. 269.
***

"While recognizing, to its fullest extent, the great power and prestige of a flourishing publishing house, and the great risk a writer runs in opposing it, I cannot bring myself to accept its invincibility, or its infallibility, or its indispensability."
—Gail Hamilton, 1870.
A Battle of the Books, 1870, pp. 281—282.
***

"Let me suggest that you print your own book: if there is any success, *you* get it; if failure, you *get* it; even this will be good discipline."
Wolstan Dixey, 1888.
The Trade of Authorship, 1888, pp. 52.
***

Encouragement and Perseverance

"Hers was not a nature to be crushed by any trouble; on the contrary, the deeper the water the better she floated."
— Darley Dale, 1889.
"The Village Blacksmith." *The Argosy*, 1889, p. 442.
***

"In shoal water you know how deep it is."
—Anonymous, 1888.
Good Housekeeping, November 10, 1888, p. 9.
***

"Keep pushing! 'Tis better than standing aside
And sighing and watching and waiting the tide.
In life's earnest battle they only prevail
Who daily march onwards and never say fail."
—Thomas E. Hill, 1891.
Hill's Manual of Social and Business Forms, 1891, p. 578.
***

"Be Patient, and don't allow impatient folks to draw away your own stock of patience. Be

Patient."
—Anonymous, 1892.
Good Housekeeping, June, 1892. p. 275.
***

"Patience is strength; impatience weakness. To sit quiet, even though what is going on wearies you, is a gain. Buds do not come up in a day, and if you wait you may find flowers where a little while ago you thought it was all barren waste."
—Anonymous, 1881.
Arthur's Home Magazine, January, 1881, p. 49.
***

"A great, strong heart is never overcome. It finds its own resources, and falls back into its own possibilities."
—E. Chapin, 19th-century.
The National Orator, 1859, p. 171.
***

"It is well to be kind to yourself that the world may follow in your footsteps."
—Anonymous, 1889.
Good Housekeeping, May 11, 1889, p. 5.
***

"'Do whatever your hand findeth to do,' and if your hand fails to find something in the right line, turn the job over to your head and heart."
—Anonymous, 1893.
Good Housekeeping, September, 1893, p. 115.

***

"What we truly and earnestly aspire *to be*, that in some sense we *are*. The mere aspiration, by changing the frame of mind, for the moment realizes itself."
—Mrs. Jameson, 1877.
A Commonplace Book of Thoughts and Memories, 1877, p. 104.

***

Desire

No joy for which thy hungering heart has panted,
No hope it cherishes through the waiting years,
But, if thou dost deserve it, it shall be granted;
For with each passionate wish the blessing nears.

Tune up the fine-strung instrument of thy being
To chord with thy dear hope; and do not tire;
When both, in key and rhythm are agreeing,

Lo! Thou shalt kiss the lips of thy desire.

The thing thou cravest so, waits in the distance,
Wrapped in the Silence, unseen and dumb.
'Tis thine to make it part of thy existence;
Live worthy of it —call— **and it will come.**

—Ella Wheeler Wilcox, 1887.
Frank Leslie's Illustrated Newspaper, December 10, 1887, p. 278.
***

"As gold is tried by fire, so is the mind of man by trials."
—John Stephenson, 1891.
"Building the First Horse-Car", *The Ladies' Home Journal* , May, 1891. p. 18.
***

"The environs surrounding our birth are matters of chance, but whether we are trump cards, and win the game of life, is largely due to ourselves."
—Marie B. Mueller, 1887.
"Random Thoughts." *Good Housekeeping*, December 10, 1887. p. 75.
***

"The first essential element of success…is to

have sufficient confidence in oneself to brave the criticisms —to say nothing of the witticisms— of a sceptical public."
—Thomas Stevens, 1888.
Around the World On A Bicycle, 1888, p. 3.
***

"Some problems are perchance unsolvable, but must the attempt to solve them count for nothing? We drop our plummet into the ocean—if it does not strike the bottom is our effort quite wasted? Is it not something to know that there is still a depth beyond our reach?"
—Anonymous, 1894.
The Leisure Hour, 1894. p. 63.
***

"To attain our end it is sometimes necessary to aim beyond it, as boys throw stones over an object in the water which they wish to float within reach."
—Anonymous, 1894.
"Scrip-Scrap." *The Leisure Hour*, 1894, p. 266.
***

"The glory is not in never falling, but in rising every time you fall."
—Anonymous, 1889.

Good Housekeeping, August 3, 1889, p. 157.
***

"Disappointment is the school of achievement, and the balked efforts are the very agents that help us to our purpose."
—E.H. Chapin, 1860.
Living Words, 1860, p. 303.
***

"Courageous minds are emboldened by difficulties. They even court encounter with hardship. No one knows his own strength until put to extremity. Obstacles! How often they vanish when valiantly assailed."
—W.H. Venable, 1872.
"Chips From A Teacher's Workshop." *The National Teacher*, June, 1872, p. 207.
***

"There is no education like adversity."
—Benjamin Disraeli, 1880.
Endymion, 1880, p. 276.
***

Optimism

"Hope is the yeast that causes the cup of life to bubble over."
—Anonymous, 1885.
Good Housekeeping, December 12, 1885, p. 71.
***

"Happily, there is always more wheat than there is chaff."
—P.T. Barnum, 1869.
Struggles and Triumphs: Or, Forty Years' Recollections, 1869. p. 397.
***

"Be content to do things you can and fret not because you cannot do everything."
—Anonymous, 1893.
Good Housekeeping, September, 1893, p. 148.
***

"Spend less nervous energy every day than you make."
—Anonymous, 1887.
Good Housekeeping, December 10, 1887. p. 65.
***

"Be Content. If 'a contented mind is a continual feast,' be careful not to go hungry from discontent. Be Content."
—Anonymous, 1892.
Good Housekeeping, June, 1892. p. 275.
***

"If you let trouble sit upon your soul, like a hen upon her nest, you may expect the hatching of a large brood."
—Anonymous, 1887.
"Kindling Wood: Split Fine for the Kitchen Fire."
Good Housekeeping, December 10, 1887. p. 72.
***

"Have you ever really thought what worry really is? It is simply wasted mental force. It is thought expended needlessly, so far as any good result is concerned. Let us suppose that we have some work to accomplish that it is important to do well, or which it is important to finish within a given time. Is that work improved in quality, or finished the sooner, if besides devoting strength and thought to its accomplishment, we devote additional strength and thought to the consideration of the results of failure? The useless expenditure of energy is what we call worry."

—J. West Roosevelt, 1894.
The Woman's Book: Volume I, 1894. p. 288.
***

"A banished trouble soon starves. By directing attention to uneasy feelings slight pain is nursed into a hard ache... Some there are to turn over and over a grief or misfortune as a ruminant chews its cud. They find a real enjoyment in complaints just as some are fond of attending funerals... and so keep up a morbid, miserable iteration that fixes an image in the mind which ought to be forever banished. If you cannot talk about pleasant themes, manage to leave. Refuse to dwell among shadows when there is so much sunshine in the world."
—Hester M. Poole, 1888.
Good Housekeeping, July 21, 1888. p. 121.
***

Happiness

"Her life was a happy one. Bear this in mind —and don't forget that your conditions of happiness need not necessarily be her conditions also."
—Wilkie Collins, 1872.
Poor Miss Finch. 1872, p. 653.
***

"Contentment swells a mite into a talent, and makes even the poor richer than the Indies."
—Anonymous, 1885.
Good Housekeeping, December 12, 1885.
***

"To make anyone happy… is strictly to augment his store of being, to double the intensity of his life, to reveal him to himself, to ennoble him and transfigure him."
—Henry Frédéric Amiel, 1868.
Amiel's Journal: Volume I, 1885, p. 155.
***

"Cheerfulness is the bright weather of the heart."
—Anonymous, 1885.
Good Housekeeping, November, 1885, p. 18.

***

"Carry sunshine in thine own heart, and, like the perfume in flowers, it will breathe a fragrance everywhere."
—Anonymous, 1887.
Good Housekeeping, December 10, 1887. p. 65.
***

Women

"It is only the silly and inexperienced who think ladyhood and work to be incompatible."
—Hester M. Poole, 1891.
"Avocations Open to Women." *The Ladies' Home Journal*, May, 1891. p. 4.
***

"Women too often hold the same erroneous opinions as their husbands. They fancy that pecuniary dependence involves inferiority of position. Because their husbands earn the money, and they themselves spend it; because their husbands claim to be the real owners of property, and class the wife as a recipient of favor, they let it go so, think it is so, act as if it were so.... Just as well might the rough and rocky foundation claim to be superior to the marble temple that rises upon it stately and beautiful. The foundation supports the temple, the temple does not support the foundation. The foundation is not dependent upon the temple; the temple is dependent upon the foundation. [Is the temple inferior?] The queen is dependent upon her subjects. The work she does for them is almost as intangible as the ideal woman's work, but

nobody considers the queen degraded thereby. It is because she is queen that all her realm pays tribute to her. Would her position be exalted, or would she do more for her kingdom by apprenticing herself to a linen-draper? She might, indeed, earn her wage, but she would have to give up being queen."
—Gail Hamilton, 1872.
Woman's Worth and Worthlessness, 1872. pp. 183—184.
***

"The meaning of the word *lady* is *loaf-giver*. Can there be a more acceptable priesthood than this service of love and labor —the token of hospitality—the badge of ladyhood?"
—Rayne, 1883.
What Can A Woman Do? 1883, p. 257.
***

"A woman may sit in her own quiet room, and, by her love, that brightens the homes of earth, and her faith, that lifts up human hearts to the hope of their heavenly home, she may send out influences that will not only make the world better and happier, but also help it to rise upward in its onward progress."
—Sarah Josepha Hale, 1866.
Manners, 1866, p. 16.

***

"But to rule, and not to deteriorate, they ought to be women indeed, strong-minded and strong-hearted; women of nerve and beauty, of ideas and opinions, of reasons and facts; women who can influence, and command, and control; who can rebuke and encourage; who shall sway men by that which is highest in both; who can discern and elicit the hidden power, and be hospitable to the modest thought; who can repress without wounding, befriend without patronizing, and refine without enervating; who can resist silently, perhaps, but steadfastly, the onset of popular fallacy, turn quietly aside from a false standard, and frame and fashion not so much by direct effort as by indirect influence. Such a woman need not say, "Be noble, be generous, be true," but, by reason of some subtile quality in herself, some unseen but persuasive and pervasive power, some insinuating grace and graciousness, no man brings to her anything but his best. Do you say such a woman is born, not made? Rather all women are born to be made thus. But the work needs care, and wisdom, and mental training, observing eyes and just reasoning, wide benevolence, and an infinite, delicate

sympathy... It is a work which, if not done by women, will not be done at all."
—Gail Hamilton, 1872.
Woman's Worth and Worthlessness, 1872. pp. 169—170.
***

"The perfect woman is as beautiful as she is strong, as tender as she is sensible. She is calm, deliberate, dignified, leisurely. She is gay, graceful, sprightly, sympathetic. She is severe upon occasion, and upon occasion playful. She has fancies, dreams, romances, ideas. Sometimes her skies are clear, like the cloudless blue of winter; but sometimes they are hazy and vague, like the Indian summer afternoon. She is never idle, but she sometimes seems to be. She uses her hands, but she never abuses them. She commands her children and her household after her, but she does not drudge for them. She administers the government of her kingdom, she *looketh* well to the ways of her family, but she never eats her bread in the sweat of her brow. Her mind is in every corner of her house, but her face shines chiefly where husband, and children, and friends sit in the light thereof. She organizes neatness, and order, and comfort, but they are merely the

foundations whereon rises the temple of her home, beautiful for situation, the joy of the whole earth."
—Gail Hamilton, 1872.
Woman's Worth and Worthlessness, 1872, p. 60.
***

"Women do not know how great are their privileges."
——Mrs. Annie Randall White, 1891.
Polite Society at Home and Abroad, 1891. p. 34.
***

"Women wish to be loved without a why or a wherefore; not because they are pretty, or good, or well-bred, or graceful, or intelligent, but because they are themselves."
—Henry Frédéric Amiel, 1868.
Amiel's Journal: Volume I, 1885, p. 209.
***

"Pray examine the first three chapters of Genesis carefully. The particular history of human creation is in the second chapter. You cannot fail to observe that there were care and preparation in the forming of woman which were not bestowed on man. Why was this recorded, if not to teach us that the wife was of finer mould, and destined to the more

spiritual uses —the heart of humanity…? She was the last work of creation. Every step, from matter to man, had been in the ascending scale. Woman was the crown of all."
—Sarah Josepha Hale, 1866.
Manners, 1866, p. 20.
***

"The intuitions of women are better and readier than those of men; her quick decisions without conscious reasons, are frequently far superior to a man's most careful deductions."
—W. Aikman, 19th-century.
A Dictionary of Thoughts, 1891, p. 630.
***

"The house-hold and society are the institutions most vital to the character and destiny of the nation, since the church and the government are what they are made by people trained in these primary schools of human existence; and both the home and social life in Christian lands are declared by common consent to be the province of woman."
—Anonymous, 1872.
The National Teacher, May, 1872, p. 151.
***

"God has made womanhood to be the most profound and winning representative of his love to man in the eternal life of the soul. In the whole realm where the spirit is to be lifted out of the limitations of materialistic, prudential, worldly considerations, and placed in contact with ideals of truth, beauty and love; in the sacred sphere of the home, and the more spiritual phases of the religious life; in that delicate border land where character flowers out into manners; also in the whole world of the minor economies and minute adaptations that 'make ends meet' in practical affairs; here, doubtless, woman is the invaluable instructor of childhood as well as manhood."
—A.D. Mayo, 1870.
The National Teacher, 1872, p. 262.
***

"As with the Commander of an Army, or the leader of an enterprise, so it is with the mistress of a house… She ought always to remember that she is the first and the last, the Alpha and the Omega in the government of her establishment; and that it is by her conduct that its whole internal policy is regulated."
—Mrs. Isabella Beeton, 1861.

The Book of Household Management. 1893 ed., p. 1.
***

"Society and civilization are to be determined largely by women."
—"A Country Parson" (*Nom de plume*), 1890.
Good Housekeeping, June 7, 1890, p. 57.
***

"Women will not find happiness in hostility to men even if they obtain a victory in it, which is very doubtful. Women of genuis have never hated men."
—Ouida (Louise de la Ramée), 1896.
Views and Opinions, 1896, p. 319.
***

Men

"A well-bred man is quiet in dress, respectful to women, kind to the weak, helpful to the feeble. He may not be always an especially generous or effusive man, but good breeding will tell him all the proper observances and the duty of being a conventional gentleman. He assumes a virtue if he have it not, and is courteous and tender to the old, the feeble, the humble."
—Anonymous, 1893.
Good Housekeeping, February, 1893, p. 71.
***

"A gentleman should pay great regard to physical training. The more manly arts he masters, such as rowing, boxing, swimming, skating, etc., the greater will be his development, and the more graceful will he become. It will add to his strength, and better fit him to defend himself against insult, and to protect women from ungentlemanly conduct upon the part of others."
———Mrs. Annie Randall White, 1891.
Polite Society at Home and Abroad, 1891. p. 45.
***

"The husband should be as studiously polite when at home as when in society. In fact, no man can be a true gentleman without being habitually polite and considerate at home. A chivalrous regard for a wife, and a deference to her wishes and comfort, is a sure indication of refinement, and will go far toward holding her love and allegiance."
—Mrs. Annie Randall White, 1891.
Polite Society at Home and Abroad, 1891. p. 22.
***

"My aunt …thinks him handsome and says he has the manners of a gentleman. This last is high praise from Miss Bathford. She despises the present generation of young men. "In my time," she said the other day, "I used to see young gentlemen. I only see young animals now —well-fed, well-washed, well-dressed; riding animals, rowing animals, betting animals —nothing more."
—Wilkie Collins, 1872.
Poor Miss Finch. 1872, p. 513.
***

"No man worthy of the name permits his wife or any woman in his house to perform the heavy drudgery of carrying coal and wood, caring for furnaces and stoves, moving stoves

and heavy furniture, beating carpets, and so on. But this need not be the limit of a man's usefulness about the house."
—"One of the Men Folks" (*Nom de plume*), 1889.
Good Housekeeping, February 2, 1889, p. 178.
***

"The businessman is so absorbed in money-making that he sacrifices his whole time to it. I can understand a woman falling in love with a lance or a sword, dull companions though they must have been, but it seems to me impossible for any woman to love a minting-machine."
—P.L. Ford, 1899.
The Story of An Untold Love, 1899, p. 123.
***

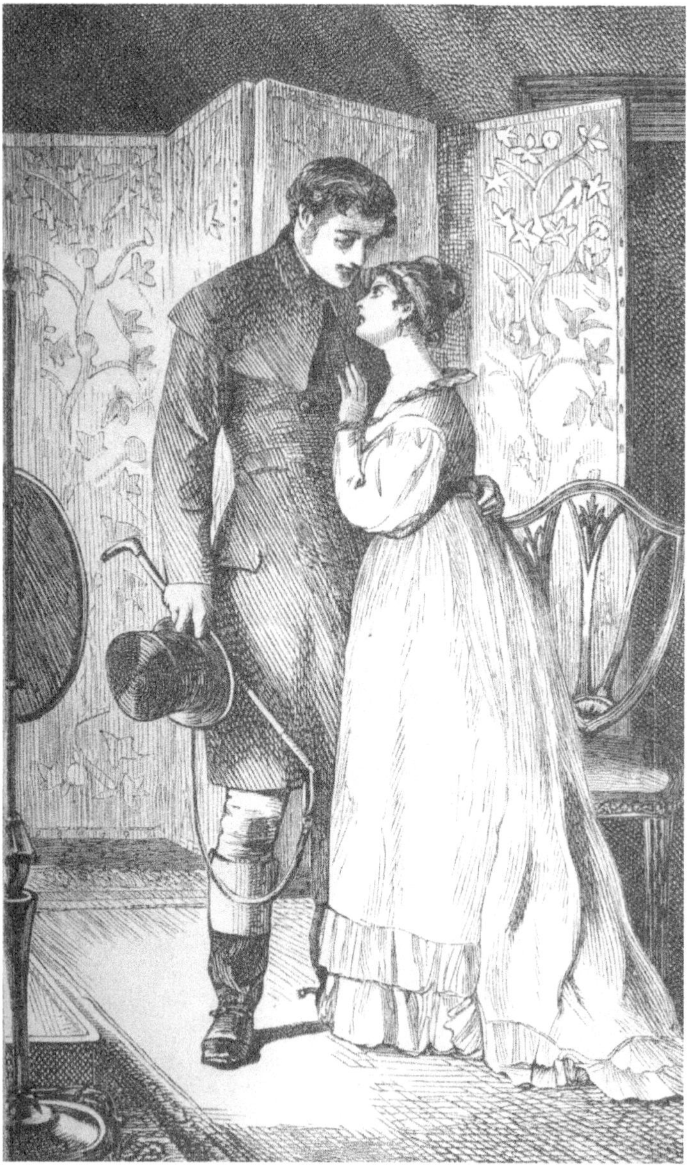

The Sexes

"It is better for men, it is better for women, that each somewhat idealize the other."
—Gail Hamilton, 1872.
Woman's Worth and Worthlessness, 1872. p. 281.
***

"He is no true man who ever treats woman with anything but the profoundest respect. She is no true woman who cannot inspire and does not take care to enforce this. Any real rivalry of the sexes is the sheerest folly and most unnatural nonsense."
—Rev. A.B. Cheales, 19th-century.
Notable Thoughts About Women, 1882, p. 293.
***

"If a woman loves her husband she is pretty sure to make him the repository of all her thoughts and feelings, and if he is worthy the confidence, his opinions and views, from a masculine standpoint, are often of the greatest assistance to her in advising her unmarried friends."
—Florine Thayer McCray, 1884.
Wheels and Whims, 1884, pp. 119—120.

***

"Much, and not too much, has been said of the duty of training men to reverance woman. But women should also be trained to reverance man; for the divine image is in both men and women, and in both alike to be revered. The too-current scoffing at the virtue of men in certain modern novels is not healthful reading for any girl; as such pictures of women as furnished by Becky Sharp are not healthful reading for any boy. The devil is a cynic, and cynicism is of the devil."
—Lyman Abbott, 1894.
The Woman's Book: *Volume I*, 1894, p. 348.
***

"Marriage is the holiest relation into which two beings can enter. It is a solemn step, but when taken with a correct appreciation of its duties, and a determination to fulfill its obligations, it seldom fails to confer happiness. Though cynics sneer, and point to the fast-multiplying records of unhappy unions, the fact still remains that the number of marriages that are blessed of heaven, is countless. It is only the loathsome debris of misery that is cast up on the surface. The

calm, majestic river flows on, and bears blessings unnumbered in its train."
—Mrs. Annie Randall White, 1891.
Polite Society at Home and Abroad, 1891. p. 346.
***

"[Mistreatment of women] is incompatible with the laws of nature. Good treatment of the female is essential to the preservation of the species."
—Albert P. Niblack, 1888.
Report of the U.S. National Museum, 1888, p. 239.
***

"Man pays deference to woman instinctively, involuntarily, not because she is beautiful, or truthful, or wise, or foolish, or proper, but because she is woman, and he can not help it. If she descends, he will lower to her level; if she rises, he will rise to her height."
—Gail Hamilton, 1872.
Woman's Worth and Worthlessness, 1872, p. 171.
***

"I know not why women should wish or clamour at once to resemble and to quarrel with man. The attitude is an unnatural one; it is sterile, not only physically but mentally."
—Ouida (Louise de la Ramée), 1896.

Views and Opinions, 1896, p. 320.
***

"There is a masculine and a feminine element in all knowledge, and a man and woman in the same study extract only what their nature fits them to see—so that knowledge can be fully orbed only when the two unite in the search and share the spoils."
—Harriet Beecher Stowe, 1866.
Pearl of Orr's Island, 1866. p. 134.
***

"Antagonism between man and woman is, of all things, unnatural. Attraction is the natural relation."
—Gail Hamilton, 1872.
Woman's Worth and Worthlessness, 1872. p. 275.
***

"Self-preservation is the first law of nature, but woman-preservation is the first law of civilization."
—Gail Hamilton, 1872.
Woman's Worth and Worthlessness, 1872. p. 248.
***

"The rank which a people occupy in the grand scale may be measured by their way of taking

their meals, as well as by treating their women."
—Mrs. Isabella Beeton, 1861.
The Book of Household Management. 1893 ed., p. 1331.
***

"In all Christian countries, men are trained to a tender care of wives, mothers, and sisters; and a chivalrous impulse to protect and provide for helpless womanhood is often stronger in men than in most women."
—Catherine E. Beecher, 1870.
Principles of Domestic Science, 1870, p. 365.
***

"No monarch has been so great, no peasant so lowly, that he has not been glad to lay his best at the feet of a woman."
—Gail Hamilton, 1872.
Woman's Worth and Worthlessness, 1872. p. 289.
***

"Though the gentlemen [at the archery meeting] shot well with yew bows, the ladies shot better with beaux yeux."
—Murray Wilkins, 1894.
The Leisure Hour, 1894, p. 540.
***

"A married man falling into misfortune is more apt to retrieve his situation in the world than a single one."
—Jeremy Taylor, 1885.
Good Housekeeping, December 12, 1885, p. 86.
***

Wanted

He
Wanted—A wife who can handle a broom,
To brush down the cobwebs and sweep up the room;
To make decent bread that a fellow can eat—
Not the horrible compound you everywhere meet,
Who knows how to broil, to fry and to roast—
Make a cup of good tea and a platter of toast;
A woman who washes, cooks, irons and stitches,
And sews up the rips in a fellow's old breeches;
And makes her own garments —an item that grows
Quite highly expensive, as everyone knows;
A common-sense creature, and still with a mind
To teach and to guide —exalted, refined;

A sort of an angel and household combined.

She

Wanted—A husband who thinks of his wife
As the help, and the pride, and the joy of his life;
Who is thoughtful to put all his garments away,
Who hangs up his slippers, brush and comb every day;
Who will bring in the water, the coal and the wood,
Nor grumble about it, nor speak harsh or rude;
Who coming to supper, as he does often, late,
Blames not the tired wife because he had to wait;
Who thinks of her numberless steps here and there,
And paying no help, grudges naught she may wear.
If a man of these qualities —blessed with a mind
That knows true from false —wants a wife, he will find
There are still a few left —wife and helpmeet combined.
—Anonymous, 1885.
Good Housekeeping, December 26, 1885, p. 122.

***

"It is recorded of a woman prominent in society and in all good works that being asked the cause of her remarkable sweetness of disposition and enjoyment of life, she answered promptly, "My husband has always been my lover."
—Mrs. Minerva Van Wyck, 1893.
Good Housekeeping, February, 1893, p. 71.
***

Love

"In every known sense of the word, a woman owns the man who loves her more than he owns her... She sees the situation, where he only sees her. She is as strong as all his strength, because his strength is hers. With whatever of power, or wisdom, or renown he is endowed, she also becomes posessed, and no enlargement of his borders diminishes one iota of his dependence on her for the ability to enjoy them. If there is any difference, the supreme control... is hers."
—Gail Hamilton, 1872.
Woman's Worth and Worthlessness, 1872. pp. 158-159.
***

"Love is the golden key that unlocks all souls."
—Rev. A.D. Mayo, 1872.
"The Spirit of School Discipline." *The National Teacher*, February, 1872, p. 44.
***

"The sound of a kiss is not so loud as that of a cannon, but its echo lasts a deal longer."
—Oliver Wendell Holmes, 1859.

The Professor at the Breakfast-Table, 1859, chapter 11.
***

"Great love alone is timeless amid change."
—Phillip Marston, 1894.
The Leisure Hour, 1894, p. 336.
***

"There is no slavery so abject as the slavery of a man to the woman he loves. Abject, for it goes behind his will and possesses the whole man. And the more a man he is, the more strong, and bright, and free, the more thorough is his enthrallment."
—Gail Hamilton, 1872.
Woman's Worth and Worthlessness, 1872. p. 158.
***

"Happiness does away with ugliness, and even makes the beauty of beauty. The man who doubts it, can never have watched the first gleams of tenderness dawning in the clear eyes of one who loves; —sunrise itself is a lesser marvel."
—Henry Frédéric Amiel, 1868.
Amiel's Journal: Volume I, 1885, p. 155.
***

"True love is that which ennobles the personality, fortifies the heart, and sanctifies the existence. And the being we love must not be mysterious and sphinx-like, but clear and limpid as a diamond; so that admiration and attachment may grow with knowledge."
—Henry Frédéric Amiel, 1880.
Amiel's Journal: Volume II, 1895, p. 324.
***

"[F]or the one we truly love we entertain at once the highest respect, the deepest reverence, the most tender kindness and the most intense sympathy; and our keenest approbativeness is experienced in relations to that one. In that one we see the heights and depths of real beauty and genuine purity; toward that one we are peculiarly and irresistibly attracted, as iron is drawn to a magnet."
—Lyman B. Sperry, 1900.
Husband and Wife, 1900. pp. 72-73.
***

Home

"This is the true nature of home -- it is the place of Peace... it is a sacred place, a vestal temple, watched over by Household Gods, before whose faces none can come but those whom they can receive with love, -- so far as it is this... so far it vindicates the name and fulfills the praise of home."
—John Ruskin, 1878.
Pearls of Wisdom for Young Ladies, 1878, p. 41.
***

"Home is the blossom of which heaven is the fruit."
—Anonymous, 1896.
Good Housekeeping, January, 1896, p. 47.
***

"Love and home: these seem inseparable ideas. As regards humanity, they began together; nor can we think of one thing without bringing up some smile or sigh of the other to delight or sadden us: thus memory, or consciousness, proves us to be true human beings."
—Sarah Josepha Hale, 1866.
Manners, 1866, p. 13.

***

"The hearth is home."
—Richard Jefferies, 1885
After London, 1885, chapter 14.
***

"In song and story, from time indefinite, the family fireside has been immortalized as the focus around which have clustered the dearest attractions of our homes."
—Mrs. M.H. Faris, 1889.
Good Housekeeping, January 19, 1889, p. 135.
***

"Have nothing in your houses that you do not know to be useful, or feel to be beautiful."
—William Morris, 19th-century.
Hopes and Fears for Art: Five Lectures Delivered in Birmingham, London and Nottingham, 1878—1881, 1882, p. 108.
***

"The name of one of our dearest possessions, "home," is a general one that applies to infinite varieties. Among the many millions of homes in the world no two are exactly alike."
—George K. Holmes, 1896.

"Home: The Dearest of All Earthly Possessions."
Good Housekeeping, January, 1896, pp. 1—2.
***

"The home is the foundation of all good things."
—Mrs. Annie Randall White, 1891.
Polite Society at Home and Abroad, 1891, p. 17.
***

"Every person must have a home of some sort, and it need not necessarily be a home as we commonly have it in mind... It may be a gypsy camp, moving from day to day, or a camp of perambulating cowboys whose only covering under the stars is their blankets, whose kitchen is a covered wagon and a small hole in the ground, where the fire is protected from the wind, and the remainder of whose home is bounded by the horizon for the time being. So is a lumberman's camp a home, or a camp of miners, or of railroad builders. The hermit's log hut in the wilderness is his home. The crowded tenement house in the city, the monotonous rows of "brown-stone fronts," and of factory dwellings, a tenement house that has risen to the dignity of a flat, a loft over a stable, the attic of a warehouse, steamboats and ships, hotels and boardinghouses —all these are or may be homes, and so are the fisherman's hut by the seashore, the slab-shanty of the charcoal burner, and the canal boat. The home of a tramp was a barn last night, it will be under a pine tree tonight. A man in Washington D.C. had his home in a tree for several years.

Indeed, the home may be almost anywhere and everywhere —in the crowded, noisy, dirty city; in the beautiful village, with its green lawns and shade trees and dwellings that suggest comfort, at least, and happiness, or it may be out in the country in a pretty valley, or out in the broad prairie in a region of farms."
—George K. Holmes, 1896.
"Home: The Dearest of All Earthly Possessions."
Good Housekeeping, January, 1896, pp. 1—2.
***

"The ownership of a home hinders migration, and civilization has not yet proceeded far enough to do away with migration as a means of bettering one's condition. Generally real estate is not readily sold without sacrifice, and men do not want to own their homes, under the circumstances, until they reach a situation where they do not object to having such an anchor upon their movements as the ownership of a home."

—George K. Holmes, 1896.
"Home: The Dearest of All Earthly Possessions."
Good Housekeeping, January, 1896, p. 3.
***

"Home! Where in our language shall we find a word of four letters that stirs all the sweet pulses of life like this of home, —Our Home? Pehaps you think of love, the master-passion, as it has been styled, of human nature. But human love owes its beginning and its perfection to its precursor, *home*. Eden, the divinely prepared abode of the first of our race, was planted before woman was created: with her came love. The home for the bride was made, and adorned with all the wealth of nature's loveliness, before the Lord God drew out, from the *carbon* of man's flesh and bones, the pure diamond of feminine purity and beauty, and light of moral perfectness, which he enshrined in the form of woman."
—Sarah Josepha Hale, 1866.
Manners, 1866, p. 20.
***

"We require from buildings two kinds of goodness: first, the doing their practical duty well: then that they be graceful and pleasing in doing it."

—John Ruskin, 1858
Stones of Venice, 1858, p. 35.
***

"It is in the home, above all other places, that the true man or woman will strive to please and soothe."
—Mrs. Minerva Van Wyck, 1893.
Good Housekeeping, February, 1893, p. 71.
***

Time

"Lost, yesterday, somewhere between sunrise and sunset, two golden hours, each set with sixty diamond minutes. No reward is offered, for they are gone forever."
—Horace Mann, 19th-century.
Bancroft's Fifth Reader, 1885. p. 146.
***

"What one of us respectable citizens can be said to STEAL? Well, wouldn't the definition of that word be the taking from one what one valued…? I only know I would as soon have my pocket picked as my day, and as soon lose my precious money as my precious time. Those hangers-on and long sitters, who cannot borrow a sleeve pattern without giving up the afternoon to it, break the eighth [commandment] in the decalogue to my thinking, and make the sufferers annihilate the sixth."
—Ruth Hall, 1887.
Good Housekeeping, October 15, 1887. p. 283.
***

"*Punctuality* is another virtue which must be cultivated by all who would succeed in any

calling, whether lofty or humble… He who needlessly breaks his appointment shows that he is as reckless as the waste of the time of others as of his own."
—Anonymous, 1885.
Bancroft's Fifth Reader, 1885, pp. 31—32.
***

"One of the most important lessons to be learned in life is the art of economizing time… Lost wealth may be replaced by industry, lost knowledge by study, lost health by temperance or medicine, but lost time is gone forever."
—Anonymous, 1885.
Bancroft's Fifth Reader, 1885. p. 146.
***

"It is said that in the Mint the sweepings of the floor of the gold-working room are melted and coined. Learn from this the nobler economy of time: glean up its golden dust; economize with the utmost care those raspings and parings of existence, those leavings of days and bits of hours, — so valueless singly, so inestimable in the aggragate, —which most persons sweep out into the waste of life, and you will be rich in leisure."

—Anonymous, 1885.
Bancroft's Fifth Reader, 1885. p. 148.
***

"Successful merchants who have made great fortunes have usually done so not by one fortunate stroke of business, but by constant attention to small matters, and by carefully looking after little sums of money, which other people would not think worth troubling about. This is how we should deal with time, not thinking even a fragment too small to be put to use."
—Anonymous, 1881.
"On the Use of Time." *Arthur's Illustrated Home Magazine*, January, 1881, p. 22.
***

"The small stones that fill up the crevices are almost as essential to the firm wall as the great stones; and so the wise use of spare time contributes not a little to the building up of a man's mind in good proportions, and with strength. If you really prize mental culture, or are sincerely anxious to do a good thing, you *will* find time, or *make* time for it, sooner or later, however engrossed with other employments. A failure to accomplish it can

only prove the feebleness of your will, not that you lacked time for execution."
—Anonymous, 1885.
Bancroft's Fifth Reader, 1885. p. 148.
***

"It is good to have something that is sacred to us, even if it be only in the distinction of time, that there should be holy hours, when heaven comes down to earth, and guardian spirits are so near that we can almost hear the fluttering of their wings."
—Rev. Henry M. Field, 1896.
"Heaven Lies about Us In Our Infancy: Heaven Lies About Us Still." *Good Housekeeping*, January, 1896, p. 9.
***

"Don't you know how hard it is for some people to get out of a room after their visit is really over? They want to be off, and you want them to be off, but they don't know how to manage it. One would think they had been built in your parlour or study, and were waiting to be launched. I have contrived a sort of ceremonial inclined plane for such visitors, which being lubricated with certain smooth phrases, I back them down, metaphorically speaking, stern-foremost, into

their 'native element,' the great ocean of out-doors."
—Oliver Wendell Holmes, 1875.
The Autocrat of the Breakfast Table, 1875, p. 19.
***

History

"Everything that exists has its origin in the past."
—Alexandre Dumas, 1861.
"A Few Words to the Reader." *Garibaldi: An Autobiography.* London: 1861. p. 7.
***

"Grand temples are built of small stones and great lives made up of trifling events."
—Anonymous, 1885.
Good Housekeeping, November, 1885, p. 18.
***

"A gold digger's life has an inevitable monotony, the object and the interest are always the same; but in digging for history the results are ever varying… Every day there is a new light on the past, a new clue to the work; unlooked for interests turn up, and in no matter is it truer than it is in the unexpected that happens."
—W.M. Flinders Petrie, 1886.
"A Digger's Life." *The English Illustrated Magazine*, March, 1886, p. 440.
***

"Archaelogy is not only the handmaid of

history, it is also the conservator of art."
—Lord Lytton, 1869
Speeches. XXXIV The Archealogical Congress, Aug 2, 1869.
***

"The past is our wisest and best instructor. In its dim and shadowy outlines we may, if we will, discern in some measure those elements of wisdom which should guide the present and secure the welfare of the future."
—Frederick Douglass, 1889.
"The Great Agitation: Fifth Paper —Reminiscences." *The Cosmopolitan.* August, 1889. p. 376.
***

"I would define man as the animal that delights in antiquities."
—William Cullen Bryant, 1890.
"Wayside Literary Litter." *Good Housekeeping.* June 21, 1890. p. 75.
***

"It is a great advance in civilization to be able to describe the common facts of life, and perhaps, if we were to examine it, we should find that it was at least an equal advance to wish to describe them."
—Walter Bagehot, 1872.

Physics and Politics, 1899 ed., p. 131.
***

"It is well to know that the harvest gathered in the fields of the past is to be brought home for the use of the present."
—Anonymous, 1886.
Good Housekeeping, June 12, 1886. p. 71.
***

"From my earliest boyhood, ancient wearing apparel, old household and kitchen utensils, and antique furniture, have appealed to me with peculiar force, telling facts and relating incidents to me in such a plain, homely but graphic manner of the every-day life of our ancestors, that I look upon them more as text-books than as curiosities; for it is only by the light of truth reflected from these objects that we are enabled to. . . pierce the. . . fiction with which the perspective of years surrounds the commonest objects of those remote times."
—Dan C. Beard, 1889.
"Six Feet of Romance." *The Cosmopolitan.* July, 1889. p. 226.
***

"We think that the age in which we live is *the* age; that the people among whom we move

are the favored o the earth, that our ways are the best, that our methods are the nearest allied to those of omniscience, that the crisis we face is the most momentous. As matter of fact, crises are as regular in the history of nations as the rising of the sun and the going down thereof."
—Joseph Howard Jr., 1888.
"A Few Facts About Elections." *The Cosmopolitan.* November, 1888. p. 53.
***

"It is but a short journey across the isthmus of Now."
—Anonymous, 1885.
Good Housekeeping, December 12, 1885, p. 71.
***

Memory

"Nothing improves the memory like practice."
—Walter R. Houghton, 1889.
American Etiquette and Rules of Politeness, 1889, p. 81.
***

"It is a most excellent practice to commit accurately to memory passages of undoubted superiority in either poetry or prose. There are two principal benefits to be derived from this. First the mind is stored with the best and greatest ideas clothed in the most appropriate words, and is thereby necessarily improved perpetually, for we can not repeatedly contemplate perfect models without being influenced by them. It is, moreover, a pure pleasure to feel that we have at command the very essence of a book."
—W.H. Venable, 1872.
"Something About Libraries, Books, and Reading.", Venable, W.H. *The National Teacher*. October, 1872, p. 381.
***

"How much in… a poem that you really did feel admirable and lovely on a first reading, passes away, if you do not give it a further

and much better reading —passes away utterly, like a sweet sound or an image on the lake, which the first breath of wind dispels! If you could only fix that image, as the photographers do theirs, so beautifully, so perfectly! And you can do so. Learn it by heart, and it is yours forever."
—Vernon Lushington, 1885.
"On Learning Pieces By Heart." *Bancroft's Fifth Reader*, 1885. p. 40.
***

"A good plan to adopt in reading is to mark and commit to memory the most beautiful thoughts met. The advantages of such a course are, that it strengthens the memory, and stores the mind with worthy ideas which mold the life; they also make the memory a valuable storehouse from whence they can draw for future use."
—Annie Randall White, 1891.
Polite Society at Home and Abroad, 1891. p. 436.
***

Education

"The true university of these days is a collection of books."
—Thomas Carlyle, 1871.
The Collected Works of Thomas Carlyle, 1871, p. 306.
***

"One must spend time in gathering knowledge to give it out richly."
—Edmund Clarence Stedman, 1885.
Poets of America, 1885, p. 327.
***

"The inspiration of the true scholar comes from the vast realms of knowledge which lie before him."
—Anonymous, 1872.
The National Teacher, March, 1872. p. 103.
***

"We hear it said that general society —the *world*, as it is called— and a public school, are excellent educators; because in one the man, in the other the boy, "finds, as the phrase is, his own level." He does not; he finds the

level of others. *That* may be good for those below mediocrity, but for those above it *bad*: and it is for those we should most care; for if once brought down in early life by the levelling influence of numbers, they seldom rise again, or only partially. Nothing so dangerous as to be perpetually measuring ourselves against what is beneath us, feeling our superiority to that which we force ourselves to assimilate to. This has been the perdition of many a school-boy and many a man."
—Mrs. Jameson, 1877.
A Commonplace Book of Thoughts and Memories, 1877, p. 114.
***

"The true aim of education is to prepare the mind to think the truth, the heart to enjoy it, the will to purpose it, and the hand to perform it."
—Anonymous, 1872.
The National Teacher, April, 1872, p. 136.
***

"No one can know or think too much, or act too well."
—W.H. Venable, 1872.

"Chips From A Teacher's Workshop." *The National Teacher*, June, 1872, p. 207.
***

"In education the state has undertaken to supplant the family. And the matter of the whole mental training of the young has been more and more turned over to the public school. The state is wholly inadequate to this work, for the reason that nothing can supply in tender years the place of a home intellectual atmosphere in the formation of the habits of children. If they are accustomed to see books, or to hear at table intelligent conversation about the world of men and things reported in books and periodicals and newspapers, they easily form a taste for going to the sources that will inform or interest or amuse them. They will not look upon reading as a task but as the pleasure it is."
—Charles Dudley Warner, 1896.
"Literature in the Home" *Good Housekeeping,* January, 1896. p. 10.
***

"In this nineteenth century, when education is a universal thing and the development of the intellect is considered a paramount object we are not content to know facts merely, as our

ancestors were, but we must inquire into the whys and wherefores. In former times, if a child studied mathematics, all that was required was that the "rules" should be committed to memory, to be used when wanted. Now, however, learning rules by rote does not suffice, except, perhaps, in the crudest of the backwoods' educational institutions. The pupil is now expected not only to know the fact that the two acute angles of a right-angled triangle are equal to one right angle, but also to know, and to be able to explain, *why* they are so."
—George Arnold, 1858.
The Sociable, 1858, p. 319.
***

"Remember that education like some other things, does not consist in the multitude of things a man possesses."
—Timothy Titcomb, 1860
The Connecticut Common School Journal and Annals of Education, May, 1860, p. 147.
***

"Some men do not try to win highly educated women because they are abashed by a sense of their own inferiority."
—P.L. Ford, 1899.

The Story of An Untold Love. 1899, p. 122.
***

"No one who resolutely sets to work to obtain an education need be apprehensive that he must fail for want of external advantages... Silvio Pellico, shut up for ten years in prison, added daily not only to his power of thought and imagination, but also to his stock of knowledge. His opportunities for acquisition and culture were exceedingly limited, but he made the best of adversity, and out of that best we have one of the masterpieces of literature, "My Prisons."
—W.H. Venable, 1872.
"Chips From A Teacher's Workshop." *The National Teacher*, June, 1872, p. 207.
***

"The non-observant man goes to Europe, and, upon returning, has nothing to tell except that he was sea-sick on the Atlantic, and that there are chalk-cliffs at Dover. You ask him concerning this and that interesting thing in London or Paris, and his only reply is, "I saw it, —I heard it, —but *didn't take particular notice.*" The man of sharpened perceptions and attentive habit, on the other hand, reaps a harvest of information from every field he

visits."
—W.H. Venable., 1872.
The National Teacher, June, 1872, p. 206.
***

Health

"The body is the temple of the soul; the shrine of the spirit. To care for it and preserve it in its highest perfection is the duty of every man and woman."
—Annie Randall White, 1891.
Polite Society at Home and Abroad, 1891. p. 403.
***

"First, when [Athena] wants to make Penelope bright and beautiful, to do away with the signs of her waiting and her grief. 'Then Athena thought of another thing; she laid her into deep sleep, and loosed all her limbs, and made her taller, and made her smoother, and fatter, and whiter than sawn ivory; and breathed ambrosial brightness over her face; and so she left her and went up to heaven.' Fresh air and sound sleep at night, young ladies! You see you may have Athena for lady's maid whenever you choose."
—John Ruskin, 1869.
The Queen of the Air, 1869. p. 43.
***

"Sleep is the best stimulant, a nervine safe for all to take."
—Anonymous, 1885.
Good Housekeeping, November, 1885, p. 18.
***

"Nature alone cures, what nursing has to do… is put the patient in the best position for nature to act upon him."
—Florence Nightingale, 1860.
Notes on Nursing, 1860, p. 191.
***

"The very first canon of nursing, the first and the last thing upon which a nurse's attention must be fixed, the first essential to the patient, without which all the rest you can do for him is as nothing, with which I had almost said you may leave all the rest alone is this: TO KEEP THE AIR HE BREATHES AS PURE AS THE EXTERNAL AIR, WITHOUT CHILLING HIM."
—Florence Nightingale, 1860.
Notes on Nursing, 1860, p. 8.
***

"A cheerful face is nearly as good for an invalid as healthy weather."
—Anonymous, 1885.

Good Housekeeping, November, 1885, p. 18.
***

"Mirth has an hygienic value [for preventing disease] that can hardly be overrated… Joy has been called the sunshine of the heart, yet the same sun that calls forth the flowers of a plant is also needed to expand its leaves and ripen its fruits; and without the stimulus of exhilarating pastimes perfect bodily health is as impossible as moral and mental vigour."
—Anonymous, 1883.
The Sanitary Record, July 15, 1883, p. 23.
***

"What doctor possesses such curative resources as those latent in a spark of happiness or a single ray of hope?… Health is the first of all liberties, and happiness gives us the energy which is the basis of health."
—Henry Frédéric Amiel, 1868.
Amiel's Journal: Volume I, 1885, p. 155.
***

"The reason the birds and wild creatures are so comfortably content [in winter] is because they are prepared for the weather, their clothing is not only soft and warm, but fits them perfectly, without interfering with their

movements. Take a lesson from them, girls, dress as becomingly as you choose, the birds always do that, but do not wear thin-soled shoes or anything that is uncomfortable; wrap up warm and you can enjoy yourself out of doors in the coldest weather just as well as the birds. The cold winds will only bring the roses to your cheeks, and the keen, invigorating air, health and suppleness to your body."
—Lina Beard and Adelia Beard, 1895.
The American Girls' Handy Book, 1895. pp. 334-335.
***

"Good health depends more upon peace of mind, than upon powders or pills."
—K.H.T., 1893.
Good Housekeeping, February, 1893, p. 101.
***

Imagination

"The imagination is the secret and marrow of civilization."
—Henry Ward Beecher, 1887.
Proverbs from Plymouth Pulpit, 1887, p. 31.
***

"Imagination is not a wild guessing, but simply the application on another scale of *ideas already clearly defined*, just as we compute the distance to the stars from measurements made on earth."
—Wolstan Dixey, 1888.
The Trade of Authorship, 1888, p. 80.
***

I built me a castle in Dreamland,
A castle fair to see,
I built it with spire and turret,
And it stood beside the sea;
And all day long the bright waves
Rolled up to the happy shores,
And all day the south wind,
Came in through the open doors.

I planted a garden in Dreamland
Around my castle fair,

I filled it with roses and lilies
And flowerets sweet and rare;
All the live day long they nodded
Their heads to the dancing breeze.
"Ah! Who ever saw," I said to myself,
"Such wondrous flowers as these!"

I hung in the halls of my castle
Pictures rare and fine,
Painted by grand old masters,
In the far off golden time;
And I used to gaze on the pictures,
Till life with sorrow and care,
Seemed distant and faint as the cloudlets,
Floating away up there.

Oh, beautiful, beautiful castle!
I know you were only a dream,
And though you vanished as dew-drops
Before the sun's bright beam,
Yet the joy I had in my castle
Will never vanish for me,
And God I thank for my castle,
My castle beside the sea.
—M.C. Schouler, 1873.
The Ladies' Repository, 1873, p. 366.
***

"Cold and cynical observers may make light of these things as idle dreams. But life is made up of dreams. 'We are such things as dreams are made of.' Instead of throwing them off, he is wise who will cling to them and wrap them close about him."
—Rev. Henry Field, 1896
"Good Housekeeping." January, 1896, p. 9.
***

"The imagination is the most active and the least susceptible of fatigue of all the faculties of the human mind; its more intense exercise is tremendous, and sometimes unsettles the reason; its repose is only a gentle sort of activity; nor am I certain that it is ever quite unemployed, for even in our sleep it is still awake and busy, and amuses itself with fabricating our dreams."
—William Cullen Bryant, 1884.
The Life and Work of William Cullen Bryant, 1884, p. 6.
***

"Men speak of dreaming as if it were a phenomenon of night and sleep. They should know better. All results achieved by us are self-promised, and self-promises are made in dreams awake."

—Lewis Wallace, 1880.
Ben-Hur, 1884 ed., p. 341.
***

Art

"Take that floral gable; you don't suppose that the man who built Stone Henge could have built that, or that the man who built that *would* have built Stonehenge? Do you think an old Roman would have liked such a piece of filigree work? Or that Michael Angelo would have spent his time in twisting these stems of roses in and out? Or, of modern handicraftsmen, do you think a burglar, or a brute, or a pickpocket could have carved it? Could Bill Sykes have done it? Or the Dodger, dextrous with finger and tool? You will find in the end, that *no man could have done it but exactly the man who did it*; and by looking closely at it, you may, if you know your letters, read precisely the manner of man he was.

Now I must insist on this matter, for a grave reason. Of all facts concerning art, this is the one most necessary to be known, that, while manufacture is the work of the hands only, art is the work of the whole spirit of man; and as that spirit is, so is the deed of it; and by whatever power of vice or virtue any art is produced, the same vice or virtue it reproduces and teaches. That which is born

of evil begets evil; and that which is born of valor and honor, teaches valor or honor."
—John Ruskin, 1869.
The Queen of the Air, 1869, p. 111.
***

"Fix, then, this in your mind as the guiding principle of all right and practical labor, and source of all healthful life energy —that your art is to be the praise of something that you love. It may only be the praise of a shell or a stone; it may be the praise of a hero; it may be the praise of God; your rank as a living creature is determined by the height and breadth of your love; but, be you small or great, what healthy art is possible to you must be the expression of your true delight in a real thing, better than the art."
—John Ruskin, 1878.
Pearls of Wisdom for Young Ladies, 1878, p. 97.
***

"To be thoroughly *in earnest*, intensely in earnest in all my thoughts and in all my actions, whether *in* my profession or *out* of it, became my single one idea. And I honestly believe herein lies the secret of my success in life. I do not believe that any great success in any art can be achieved without it… Art is an

absolute mistress; she will not be coquetted with or slighted; she requires the most entire self-devotion and she repays it with grand triumphs."
—Charlotte Cushman, 1874.
Charlotte Cushman: Her Life, Letters and Memories, 1878. p. 263.
***

"[A]s all lovely art is rooted in virtue, so it bears fruit of virtue."
—John Ruskin, 1869.
The Queen of the Air, 1869, p. 114.
***

Fashion

"It is better to be slightly out of the fashion than to spoil one's good looks."
—J.R. Stitson, 1900.
The Human Hair: Its Care and Preservation, 1900, p. 152.
***

"It may seem absurd, but not the least part of my eagerness that night was to see you in evening dress. If I had not loved you already, I should have done so from that meeting; and although you are dear to me for many things besides your beauty, I understand why men love you so deeply who know nothing of your nature."
—P.L. Ford, 1899.
The Story of An Untold Love. 1899, p. 118.
***

"Dress, then, is something more than necessity of climate, something better than condition of comfort, something higher than elegance of civilization. Dress is the index of conscience, the evidence of our emotional nature. It reveals, more clearly than speech expresses, the inner life of heart and soul in a

people, and also the tendencies of individual character."
—Sarah Josepha Hale, 1866.
Manners, 1866, p. 39.
***

"Since the first garment of all, clothes have been knowledge, influence, and expression, and house and home to the wearer. They have taught him his first conscious idea; they were his first link with this outer scene; they first made him realise that he was a personage in the world of vaguely apprehended forms, of which his unpracticed senses partially informed him. A life without clothes, not to mention its other inconveniences, would, we verily believe, be a life without thought."
—Anonymous, 1865.
Blackwood's Edinburgh Magazine, April, 1865, p. 425.
***

"In all times when beauty and comfort are studied, corsets will undoubtedly be worn, and there are many reasons why they should be."
—Madame Roxey A. Caplin, 1864.
Health and Beauty: Women and Her Clothing, 1864. p. 82.

***

"The principal writers upon the subject of Corsets have been... men, who, great as is their knowledge of *their* part of the question, certainly know nothing of ours; and hence what they have written has been almost entirely without practical utility."
—Madame Roxey A. Caplin, 1864.
Health and Beauty: Women and Her Clothing, 1864. p. viii.
***

"Yes, the ladies do choose to be shaped by the staymaker, and in these days of wondrous corsets the ladies are, as usual, right... they will follow their own sweet will... Even in the earliest periods some attempt was made to shape the figure by swathing and supporting bands... When any active exercise is in progress, as running for example, the first thing the athlete does is to tighten his waist-belt, this gives the support required and materially aids his efforts... [T]here is now so large a choice of corsets that the most opposite figures can be suited with perfectly fitting corsets."
—"The Silkworm" (*nom de plume*), 1882.
Myra's Threepenny Journal, June 1, 1882, p. 105.

***

"The best corset makers have as many as seven or eight different styles, fitted to as many different figures."
—Helena Rowe, 1893.
"The Art of Shopping." *Good Housekeeping*, February, 1893, p. 69.
***

"That the wearing of corsets is a gain to many women is evident enough from the fact that they are worn under conditions in which the wearers are regardless of mere personal appearance. For instance, we may cite the working peasant-women, unmarried as well as married, of France, Switzerland, the Tyrol, Austria and Hugary, etc., etc., who wear stays during the performance of very laborious work, yet who, one could not suppose, would do this if their stays interfered with their comfort or movements.

Another example of the same fact is illustrated by the very poor workingwomen of our own nation [America], who, when obliged to sell their clothes, or, when these hang about them in rags, still, as a rule, stick to the use of stays."
—C.S. Roy, M.D., 1889.

"The Physiological Bearing of Waist-Belts and Stays.", 1889.
***

"[P]roperly constructed, corsets are, as articles of dress, the most beneficial that can be constructed."
—Madame Roxey A. Caplin, 1864.
Health and Beauty: Women and Her Clothing, 1864. p. 82.
***

"Were the gift given us to look a bit into the future, what should we probably find the middle-of-the-twentieth-century girl wearing on her wheel —bloomers, very short tunics, or trouserettes and similar abominations in the sight of grace and sweet femininity? Not if she is the direct descendant of her nineteenth-century grandmother, who here in these United States, spite of talk to the contrary, and of the efforts of fashion, still sticks to her traditions and her skirts. Long may they wave, the petticoats in modest ankle-length folds of brown cloth or gray, since those are the best colors for cycling! In time may petticoats triumph over the women who fail to recognize that bloomers are too great a sacrifice for our sex ever to make, and that in

skirts only can they maintain at once in the eyes of men their womanliness and their independence."
—Mary L. Bisland, 1896.
Bisland, Mary L. *Godey's Magazine,* April, 1896, pp. 385—388.
***

Food

"Tell me what thou eatest, and I will tell thee what thou art."
—Brillat Savarin, 1886.
"The Influence of the Kitchen." *Good Housekeeping*, June 26, 1886. p. 93
***

"Dinner will no doubt be boiling in the pot at the crack of doom! Our daily necessities go on through all tribulation and despair."
—Anonymous, 1889.
"Apples of Gold in Pen Pictures." *Good Housekeeping*, August 3, 1889, p. 160.
***

"Every lover of good butter ought to look with contempt upon the originators of the miserable compounds of oleomargarine"
—A.F.W. Neynaber, 1890.
Good Housekeeping, May 24, 1890, p. 33.
***

"I declare bad food to be at the bottom of any amount of peevishness, hot temper, family dispute, weak will-power, vitiated tastes, bad morals, and general viciousness."
—May Riley Smith, 1886.

Good Housekeeping, June 26, 1886, p. 93.
***

"Nice things are, in the main, things that are good for us, and nasty things are poisonous or otherwise injurious. That we often find the contrary the case is due, not to the provisions of nature, but to the artificial surroundings in which we live, and to the cunning way in which we flavor up unwholesome food, so as to deceive and cajole the natural palate… Our likes and dislikes are the best guide to what is good for us… Whatever is relished will prove on the average wholesome, and whatever rouses disgust will prove on the whole indigestible."
—Grant Allen, 1893.
Good Housekeeping, September, 1893, p. 139.
***

"How much of life is taken up with eating and drinking and with the struggles in order that we may eat and drink in comfort! The realm of fiction frees itself from these grosser elements. How seldom do the heroes and heroines of poetry indulge in a meal! It is doubtful whether a hearty meal has been taken in poetry since Homer's robust heroes handled the spit as deftly as the sword. With

what a gusto did they eat and drink their fill! The times have grown more refined, and your walking gentleman will pervade three volumes and never trouble you for more than a brandy-and-soda."
—Anonymous, 1894.
The Leisure Hour, 1894, p. 63.
***

Work

"The beauty of work depends on the way we meet it,—whether we arm ourselves each morning to attack it as an enemy that must be vanquished before night comes, or whether we open our eyes with the sunrise, to welcome it as an approaching friend who will keep us delightful company all day, and who will make us feel, at evening, that the day was well worth its fatigues."
—Lucy Larcom, 1898.
"The American Kitchen Magazine," January, 1898, p. 152.
***

"Those who have finished by making others think with them, have usually been those who began by daring to think with themselves."
— Thomas E. Hill, 1891.
Hill's Manual of Social and Business Forms, 1891. p. 139.
***

"Make the most of your brain and your eyes, and let no one dare tell you that you are devoting yourself to a low sphere of action."
—Anonymous, late 19th-century

Woman's Exchange Cook Book, late nineteenth-century, p. 388.
***

"Work to-day, for you know not how much you may be hindered to-morrow."
—Anonymous, 1887.
Good Housekeeping, December 10, 1887. p. 65.
***

"He who labors with the mind governs others; he who labors with the body is governed by others."
— Thomas Hill, 1891.
Hill's Manual of Social and Business Forms, 1891. p. 139.
***

"In order to have any success in life, or any worthy success, you must resolve to carry into your work a fulness of knowledge—not merely a sufficiency, but more than a sufficiency. In this respect, follow the rule of the machinists. If they want a machine to do the work of six horses, they give it nine horse power, so that they may have a reserve of three. To carry on the business of life you must have surplus power. Be fit for more than the thing you are now doing. Let every one

know that you have a reserve in yourself; that you have more power than you are now using."
— James A. Garfield, 1869
"Elements of Success—Address Delivered in Spencerian Business College, Washington D.C., June 29, 1869."
***

"There is no machinery in the world that does such valuable work as human hands, and these are regulated by the head and heart. When a painter was once commended for his fine sunsets, he was asked what he mixed his colors with, and his answer was, 'With brains, sir.'"
—Rayne, 1883.
What Can A Woman Do? 1883, p. 222.
***

"Use your brains rather than those of others."
—Anonymous, 1887.
Good Housekeeping, December 10, 1887. p. 65.
***

"'When,' said a wise man once, 'is a horse in a wretched case? Not when he cannot crow, but when he cannot run. When is a dog? Not

when he cannot fly, but when he cannot trace.'"
—Anonymous, 1894.
"Second Thoughts on Books." *Leisure Hour*, 1894, p. 46.
***

"Be Plucky. The faint-hearted rarely know what it is to win place and power. Be Plucky."
—Anonymous, 1892.
Good Housekeeping, June, 1892. p. 275.
***

"Be the architect of your own fortune."
—Osgood Bradbury, 1855.
New York Consuelo, 1855, p. 79.
***

"It is always a thankless task to sit down idly and say, 'Why doesn't some one do this or that?' Some one will do it when it is known that it will pay."
—"Daisy" *(nom de plume)*, 1886.
"From A Feminine Point of View", *The Cycle*, April 9, 1886, p. 20.
***

"Activity is not always energy... Misdirected labour is but a waste of activity."
—Anonymous, 1858.
Readings for Young Men, Merchants, and Men of Business, 1858, p. 4.
***

"Man cannot destroy material, but he may waste work... The paper which you cram into your fire and fancy out of the way *is* out of the way. It will, indeed, presently become paper again, but it is by the roundabout road of smoke and ashes, and corn and cotton. Whereas, in the tin-peddler's hands it is next door to pulp, and comes back to paper by a short cut."
—Gail Hamilton, 1874.
Twelve Miles From A Lemon, 1874, p. 24.
***

"If the untutored Irishwoman who exults over the destruction of her mistress's house and property should see herself, in consequence, at once turned out of house and home, and reduced to beggary, she would exult no more. She would see that her mistress's loss was her own. Society has become so compact and complicated that the loss is too minutely subdivided to attract Bridget's notice, but it is

none the less there, and is just as truly hers as if she bore the whole brunt of it on her shoulders."
—Gail Hamilton, 1873.
Twelve Miles From A Lemon, 1873, p. 73.
***

"If there is anything worth laboring for, it is worthy of protection…The source of supply to the laborer —viz.: capital— is as truly worthy of protection as the fountain which supplies us with water. The laborer cannot be protected when the source of his earnings is open to all kinds of attack and destruction."
—John Draper, 1887.
Shams, 1887, p. 133.
***

"Workmen and workwomen are striking everywhere for higher wages and less work, with what success it is impossible to say. Because a class of mechanics wrest from their employers ten hours' wages for eight hours' work, they are by no means successful. Because an employer secures for two dollars work which is worth three, he has not necessarily come off conquerer. The laws of trade are as uncontrollable as the laws of the sea. If either employer or employed make an

unnatural advantage in one direction, trade will restore the balance by a corresponding disadvantage in another place."
—Gail Hamilton, 1873.
Twelve Miles From A Lemon, 1873, p. 75.
***

"I know there are many men who, when a few cases of great hardship occur, and it is evident that there is an evil somewhere, think that some arrangement must be made; some law passed, or some society got up, to set all rights at once. On this subject there can be no call for any such movement; on the contrary, I fully believe that any public and strong action would do harm, and that we must be satisfied to labor in the less easy and less exciting task of gradual improvement, and abide the issue of things working slowly together for good."
—Richard Henry Dana, 1840.
Two Years Before the Mast, 1840, p. 349.
***

"[T]o speak the word that cheers and encourages some unknown toiler, to reward modest merit with welcome praise, is surely worthier than to wield the scorpion whip of a Jeffrey, wounding friend and foe alike."
—Anonymous, 1894.

"Second Thoughts on Books." *Leisure Hour*, 1894, p. 46.
***

"Your duty is to look towards your work and do the wisest, best, and most beautiful thing within you."
—Rev. A.D. Mayo, 1872.
"The Spirit of School Discipline." *The National Teacher*, February, 1872, p. 48.
***

"It takes every grade of society to make the complete whole. One class is just as necessary as the other… As in the materials that enter into the erection of the building, the foundation stones that support the superstructure down deep in the earth, while they are never seen, are nevertheless just as essential to the completion of the building as are the ornamental capstones above the windows; so, in associated labor, each grade of mind does its appropriate work. We could not dispense with either, and all should have due praise.

Each class being thus dependent one upon the other, all should labor in harmony together. The workman should guard his employer's interest. He should always be promptly on time and faithful to the last hour. He should make his work a study; he should give it thought, as thereby he renders his services so much the more valuable, and his compensation in the end so much better…

The employer, through kind and pleasant manner, may do much toward making the subordinate worthy and competent. The workman should thoroughly understand what the duty is which he is expected to perform, and he should be required pleasantly yet firmly to execute it to the letter. When once there is a definite understanding on his part as to what is explicitly required, it is not necessary that an employer use harsh means or a manner in any way discourteous in order to secure obedience to his commands. A word of encouragement will increase the harmony."

—Thomas E. Hill, 1891.
Hill's Manual of Social and Business Forms, 1891, p. 172.

***

Money

"There is a point at which thrift degenerates into meanness… Waste is, of course, a bad thing in itself, independently of the value of the thing wasted; but… who has not noticed that the effort to save money often results in a larger outlay? One often foregoes the pleasure of buying something really nice, and gets a cheap substitute, only to find that the low-priced article, which looked so serviceable, is absolutely worthless, and that the money spent on it has been simply thrown away."
—"The London Lady" (*nom de plume*), 1890. *Good Housekeeping*, May 24, 1890, p. 42.
***

"I am a strict believer in economy and frugality, but I have learned that economy is a relative, and not as many suppose, an absolute term. That which is economy for me may not be so for my neighbor, and vice versa. It is very poor economy for me to buy a round steak, out of an allowance of one dollar and then spend a large proportion of what remains to buy material for that insipid nothingness called 'Angel Food.' I find it far better to buy

a good sirloin or porter-house steak and then make a cake requiring but two eggs, which to our notion far surpasses 'Angel Food" in excellence.'
—Ida Branch Mills, 1888.
Good Housekeeping, October 13, 1888, p. 276.
***

"While it is good policy in the matter of purchasing, to avail oneself as far as possible of 'sales,' beware of 'sells,' and of goods offered much below their standard price."
—Cuno Vidal, 1889.
Good Housekeeping, January 19, 1889, p. 130.
***

Technology

"The world is rapidly increasing its facilities. The past hundred years have revolutionized our style of living, travel, and communication. Steam, electricity, the telephone and the bicycle bring time and distance greatly under man's control."
—Anonymous, 1883.
"Shall the Bicycle be used on the Sabbath?" *The Wheelman*, August, 1883. p. 369.
***

"It is always better for a man to work with his own hands to feed and clothe himself, than to stand idle while a machine works for him; and if he cannot by all the labor healthily possible to him feed and clothe himself, then it is better to use an inexpensive machine —as a windmill or watermill— than a costly one like a steam-engine, so long as we have natural force enough at our disposal."
—John Ruskin, 1869.
The Queen of the Air. 1869, p. 132.
***

"Send not for a hatchet to break open an egg with."
—Anonymous, 1896.

"Pertinent and Impertinent." *Good Housekeeping*, January, 1896, p. 19.
***

"The carpenter employs an ax and cross-cut saw on the rough log; a smoothing-plane and fine chisel on the shapen board; and finer instruments still as his work approaches completion. Each kind of material is wrought by a suitable instrument. A pine stick yields to the edge of a pen-knife; but a bar of iron must be heated and hammered into shape. Neither knife, fire nor hammer meets the sculptor's needs."
—W.H. Venable, 1872.
"The Best Laws", *The National Teacher*, May, 1872, p. 171.
***

"In every idle arm and shoulder throughout the country there is a certain quantity of force, equivalent to the force of so much fuel; and… it is mere insane waste to dig coal for our force, while the vital force is unused, and not only unused, but in being so, corrupting and polluting itself. We waste our coal, and spoil our humanity at one and the same instant."
—John Ruskin, 1869.
The Queen of the Air. 1869, p. 133.
***

Politics

"He forgot to tell the people that the best citizens were sober, honest and industrious; that they were the ones who spent the least time in talking politics, and made the least noise on election days. He forgot to mention in his speeches that the shiftless, lazy and profligate people were the ones that made the most noise about elections, and complained the most about monopolies and rich men."
—John S. Draper, 1887.
Shams, 1899 ed., p. 129.
***

"There are two things that engage for the time the enthralled attention of an American multitude. One is the political fight every four years, in which half the nation does its best by every unrighteous method to 'down' the other half. The other is a champion prize-fight, in which two big, well-made brutes, try to batter each other to pieces."
—Wolstan Dixey, 1889.
The Trade of Authorship, 1889. p. 100.
***

"It is true that the wholesale exercise of electoral rights by millions of uneducated and unwashed men is a spectacle so absurd that a little more or a little less absurdity may be held not to matter very greatly. The intellectual world in political matters has voluntarily abdicated already and given its sceptre to the mob… Vapourings about the inherent 'rights of man' have been allowed to oust common-sense and logical action, and he whose contributions to the financial and intellectual power of his nation are of the largest and noblest order has no more electoral voice in the direction of the nation than the drunken navvy or the howling unit of the street-mob."
—Ouida (Louise de la Ramée), 1896.
Views and Opinions, 1896, p. 303.
***

"Theoretically, a republic is founded on the doctrine of the supremacy of the fittest; but who can say that since the days of Perikles any republic has carried out this doctrine practically? The lawyer or chemist who neglects his business to push himself to the front in political life in France is certainly not the most admirable product of French intellect; nor can it be said by any impartial

student that every President of the United States has been the highest type of humanity that the United States can produce."
—Ouida (Louise de la Ramée), 1896.
Views and Opinions, 1896, p. 306.
***

"Offenses against a free ballot are not only numerous but flagrant everywhere; but in view of the fact that, while third parties now and then crop up… as a rule, the country is divided into opposing factions, two in number, and of about equal strength… We recognize the simple fact that the chief end and aim of nineteen-twentieths of the leaders of our respective parties is office for themselves, and patronage for their friends."
—Joseph Howard Jr., 1888.
"A Few Facts About Elections." *The Cosmopolitan.* November, 1888. pp. 53—54.
***

"You can make no nation virtuous by act of parliament."
—Ouida (Louise de la Ramée), 1896.
Views and Opinions, 1896, p. 309.
***

The Company We Keep

"The brave man is an inspiration to the weak, and compels a following... Nothing is so contagious as example; we are never much good or much evil without imitators."
—Anonymous, 1887.
Good Houskeeping, December 24, 1887, p. 95.
***

"As in water face answereth to face, so the heart of man to man and woman to woman."
—Gail Hamilton, 1874.
Twelve Miles from A Lemon, 1874, p. 73.
***

"Do unto yourself what you would think it right to do for your best friend."
—Anonymous, 1893.
Good Housekeeping, September, 1893, p. 115.
***

"A lie, though it be killed and dead, can sting sometimes —like a dead wasp."
—Mrs. Jameson, 1877.
A Commonplace Book of Thoughts and Memories, 1877, p. 107.
***

"He is never alone when accompanied by noble thoughts."
—Anonymous, 1885.
Good Housekeeping, December 12, 1885.
***

"This business of conversation is a very serious matter. There are men that it weakens one to talk with an hour more than a day's fasting would do… It is better to lose a pint of blood from your veins than to have a nerve tapped."
—Oliver Wendell Holmes, 1875.
The Autocrat of the Breakfast Table, 1875, p. 6.
***

"Hasty words often rankle in the wound which injury gives, and… soft words assuage it, forgiving cures, and forgetting takes away the scar."
—Anonymous, 1885.
Good Housekeeping, November, 1885, p. 18.
***

"Trust no secrets to a friend which, if reported, would make an enemy."
—Anonymous, 1887.
Good Housekeeping, December 10, 1887. p. 65.
***

"Learn to say no; not snappishly, but firmly and respectfully."
—Anonymous, 1887.
Good Housekeeping, December 10, 1887. p. 65.
***

"To be anxious about a soul that is always snapping at you must be left to the saints of the earth; and Mary was not one of them."
—George Eliot, 1871.
Middlemarch, 1874 edition, p. 233.
***

"When narrow or obtuse people are once brought to see that it is really polite to try, in their conversation, to find out what is interesting to others, and try to make it of interest to themselves and talk of it, they are apt to overdo it and 'run it into the ground.' If well adapted and adroitly used, of course such an attempt is often productive of happy social intercourse with people who are really interesting. But to determine you have found THE subject which is sure to please your guest, to stick to that one only, to thrust it on him, never mind how he may struggle for freedom, or wish for a change, is social suicide."

—Margaret Arthur, 1887.
"Hospitality: A few of the ways in which we make guests uncomfortable." *Good Housekeeping*, October 15, 1887. p. 277.
***

"The good talker is known by what he says, and also by what he does not say."
—Anonymous, 1894.
The Leisure Hour, 1894, p. 63.
***

"The Fool hath said: 'Consider not what people say, but what they think.' Consider neither; determine which is right and go ahead; people will talk, and they who talk most think least."
—Anonymous, 1892.
Good Housekeeping, June, 1892, p. 271.
***

"It is well to know that the mission of a crank is to turn things over."
—Anonymous, 1889.
Good Housekeeping, May 11, 1889, p. 5.
***

"Show your respect for honesty in whatever guise it appears, and your contempt for dishonesty and duplicity wherever found."
—Anonymous, 1887.
Good Housekeeping, December 10, 1887. p. 65.
***

"In private watch your thoughts; in the family watch your temper; in company watch your tongue."
—Anonymous, 1887.
Good Housekeeping, December 10, 1887. p. 65.
***

"The trouble and worry and wear and tear that comes from hating people makes hating unprofitable."
—Anonymous, 1883.
Puget Sound Argus, January 27, 1883.
***

"Prejudice, like a pig pasture, is deeply rooted."
—Anonymous, 1889.
Good Housekeeping, February 16, 1889, p. 178.
***

"There are men whose friends are more to be pitied than their enemies."

—Anonymous, 1885.
Good Housekeeping, November, 1885, p. 18.
***

"The brave man is an inspiration to the weak, and compels a following."
—Anonymous, 1887.
Good Housekeeping, December 24, 1887, p. 95.
***

[About a grumbler]: "Having torn down the old structure and thrown such a quantity of cold water on his audience as to quench every spark of enthusiasm therein, he sits down to contemplate the barren waste that himself has made. To build up waste places is of course no part of his business."
—Anonymous, 1872.
The National Teacher, July, 1872. pp. 245—246.
***

A Word About Words

Ah me! These terrible little tongues of ours,
Are we half aware of their mighty powers?
Do we ever trouble our heads at all
Where the jest may strike, or the hint may fall?
The latest chirp of that "little bird,"

The spicy story "you must have heard"—
We jerk them away in our gossip rash,
And somebody's glass, of course, goes *smash!*
What fames have been blasted and broken,
What pestilent sinks have been stirred,
By a word in lightness spoken,
By only an idle word?

A sneer —a shrug— a whisper low—
They are poisoned shafts from the ambushed bow!
Shot by the coward, the fool, the knave,
They pierce the mail of the great and brave;
Vain is the buckler of wisdom and pride
To turn the pitiless points aside;

The lip may curl with a careless smile,
But the heart drips blood —drips blood the while.
Ah me! What hearts have been broken,
What rivers of blood been stirred,
By a word in malice spoken,
By only a bitter word?

A kindly word and a tender tone—
To only God is their virtue known!
They can lift from the dust the abject head,
They can turn a foe to a friend instead;
The heart close-barred with passion and pride

Will fing at their knock its portals wide,
And the hate that blights and the scorn that sears
Will melt in the fountain of childlike tears.
What ice-bound griefs have been broken,
What rivers of love been stirred,
By a word in kindness spoken,
By only a gentle word.

—Anonymous, 1889.
Good Housekeeping, February 2, 1889, p. 170.
***

Minding your own business

"How… impertinent is it to give your advice when you know nothing about the truth…"
—Florence Nightingale, 1860.
Notes on Nursing, 1860, p. 145.
***

"The tone of good company is marked by the absence of personalities. Among well-informed persons there are plenty of topics to discuss, without giving pain to anyone present."
—Anonymous, 1850
Student and Family Miscellany, 1850. p. 38.
***

"Madam Rumor is a wicked old jade."
—Anonymous, 1889.
Good Housekeeping, February 16, 1889. p. 178.
***

"To smile at the jest which plants a thorn in another's breast is to become a principal in the mischief."
—Anonymous, 1887.
Good Housekeeping, December 24, 1887, p. 95.

***

"Beware of the man of two faces."
—Anonymous, 1887.
Good Housekeeping, October 15, 1887.
***

"The tongue is not steel yet it cuts."
—Anonymous, 1885.
Good Housekeeping, November, 1885, p. 18.
***

"It is better to be able to say No, than to be able to read Latin."
—Anonymous, 1885.
Good Housekeeping, November, 1885, p. 18.
***

"True blessedness is near unto those who keep their mouths shut when the mouth ought not to be open."
—Anonymous, 1894.
Good Housekeeping, August, 1894, p. 71.
***

Miscellaneous

"I have always had a great deal of sympathy for the woman, who, after reading numerous articles on various household topics, by writers and workers of an extremely thorough type, said that she couldn't live up to all they set down as necessary, but that she tried to be 'pretty middling neat.' She was, of course, pounced upon and scored severely by many of the over-particular, but stood her ground and maintained that she was right. And I believe she was."
—Viola Fuller Miner, 1893.
Good Housekeeping, September, 1893, p. 129.
***

"The truths a man carries about with him are his tools; and do you think a carpenter is bound to use the same plane but once to use smooth a knotty board with or to hang up his hammer after it has driven its first nail?"
—Oliver Wendell Holmes, 1875.
The Autocrat of the Breakfast Table, 1875, p. 8.
***

"He was gentle only with the weak and humble. The proud and presumptuous he tore to pieces with a savage joy."
—George Parsons Lathrop.
The Cosmopolitan, July, 1889.
***

"My daintiness does not hurt you."
—Richard Jefferies, 1885.
After London. 1885. Part II, Chapter 4.
***

"Loyalty to best convictions is an important duty."
—Anonymous, 1888.
Good Housekeeping November 10, 1888, p. 9.
***

"Meanness shun and all its train; goodness seek and life is gain."
—Thomas E. Hill, 1891.
Hill's Manual of Social and Business Forms, 1891, p. 142.
***

"Certainly, the world is growing smaller, not like a withered orange but like a gem in the process of polishing."
—Anonymous, 1888.

"Housekeeping In And Among the Planets." *Good Housekeeping*, May 12, 1888. p. 3.
***

"Revolution does not insure progress."
—Anonmous, 1888.
Good Housekeeping, December 8, 1888, p. 63.
***

"It is true that there are liberties and liberties. Yonder torrent, crystal-clear, and arrow-swift, with its spray leaping into the air like white troops of fawns, is free enough. Lost, presently, amidst bankless, boundless marsh — soaking in slow shallowness, as it will, hither and thither, listless among the poisonous reeds and unresisting slime it is free also. We may choose which liberty we like — the restrain of voiceful rock, or the dumb and edgeless shore of darkened sand."
— John Ruskin, 1869.
The Queen of the Air. 1869. p. 151-152.
***

"What a picture of self-contradiction I present —and how improbable it is that I should act in this illogical way! *You* never alter your mind under the influence of your temper or your circumstances. No: you are what they

call a consistent character. And I? Oh, I am only a human being —and I feel painfully conscious that I have no business to be in a book."
—Wilkie Collins, 1872.
Poor Miss Finch. 1872, p. 603.
***

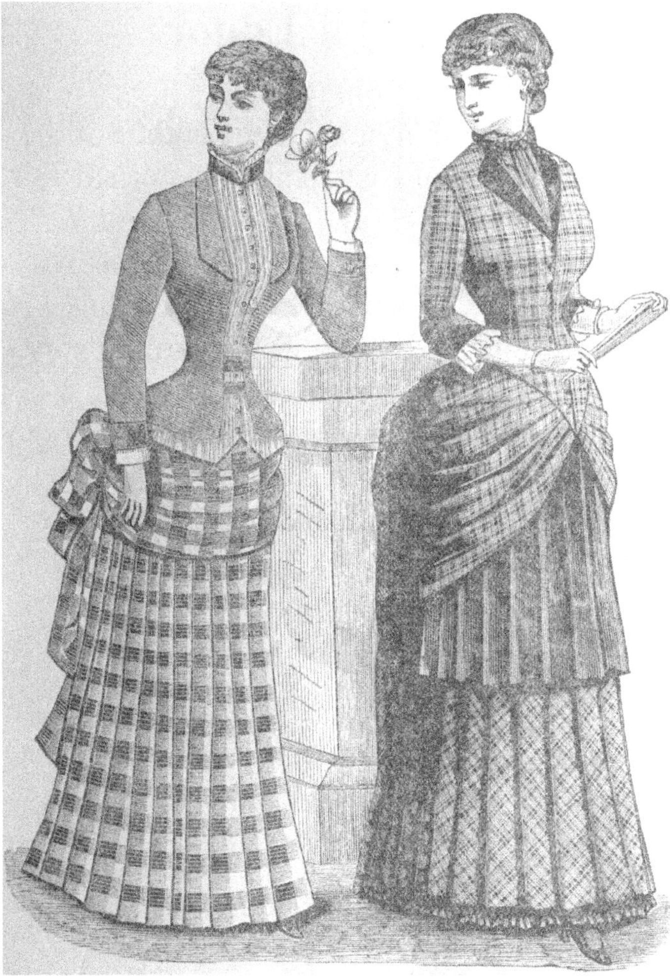

About the Editor

Sarah A. Chrisman is the author of the charming Tales of Chetzemoka historical fiction series as well as *This Victorian Life*, *Victorian Secrets*, and others. She lives in a house built in 1888, sews her own clothes, bakes her own bread in a wood-burning stove from 1901, and incorporates as many elements of Victorian culture and technology into her daily life as humanly possible. To learn more about Sarah and her books, go to www.ThisVictorianLife.com.

The Tales of Chetzemoka
By Sarah A. Chrisman

In a seaport town in the late 19th-century Pacific Northwest, a group of friends find themselves drawn together —by chance, by love, and by the marvelous changes their world is undergoing. In the process, they learn that the family we choose can be just as important as the ones we're born into. Join their adventures in *The Tales of Chetzemoka*!

http://www.thisvictorianlife.com/historical-fiction.html

Printed in Great Britain
by Amazon